More Light

Other Books by the same author

Life in the World Unseen
More about Life in the World Unseen
Here and Hereafter (originally 'The ABC of Life')
Facts
Heaven and Earth

More Light

~ further spirit communications
from
Monsignor Robert Hugh Benson

Received & Recorded by

Anthony Borgia

First published 1947
This edition 2020

Published by
Saturday Night Press Publications
England

snppbooks@gmail.com
www.snppbooks.com

ISBN 978-1-908421-42-5

www.snppbooks.com

Cover design: *Ann Harrison (SNPP) with permission to use a
painting of 'The Old Road' by Marjorie Hesford.*

Contents

Preface

In an earlier volume, *Facts*, the spirit communicator gave some account of his 'revised theology'. In this, his latest script, he returns to the theological theme with particular reference to the creeds and to certain of the miracles as narrated in the New Testament.

As a priest in earthly life, he sampled two kinds of Orthodoxy, 'one fairly free and easy-going, the other rigorous and unremitting; the first permitting private judgement upon most religious matters, the second allowing only the voice of authority to speak.'

Indulgence is asked for repeating, though the repetition seems unavoidable, that my friendship with the communicator of this book began in 1909, five years before he passed into the spirit world.

In returning to speak, he has brought with him on many occasions a host of mutual friends, the theology of most of whom has, like his own, been drastically revised.

Once again it has been my privilege to act as his earthly amanuensis, and to record further details of his 'revised theology'.

Anthony Borgia

Orthodoxy

A number of my friends of earth are still somewhat puzzled by the views which I have expressed upon the subject of Orthodoxy, by which, of course, I mean Christian Orthodoxy. Knowing one or two details of my earthly life, my friends ask, in effect, can Orthodoxy be so utterly useless as I have made it out to be in my previous writings?

They find it difficult, to say the least, to throw off completely all those old ideas which hundreds and hundreds of years of superstitious regard of traditional Orthodoxy have made so familiar, so much a part of one's natural and normal life upon earth.

The Christian religion has been codified into creeds and dogmas and doctrines whereby all men can find the true way of living upon earth, and the assurance that if they will but follow the Church's teachings they will provide for themselves adequately 'hereafter' in the spirit world, though they would not refer to their destination in such terms, but would call it 'heaven'.

My friends are a little puzzled, too, at my general attitude towards the Church (of whatever denomination), remembering that, upon my own statement, I was a priest when I lived upon earth not so very many years ago.

I have already recounted some of the details of my emergence from the mental darkness of my religious beliefs following upon my arrival in the spirit world—in a word, how I came to throw off all my orthodox ideas with such rapidity, so that I will not again go over old ground. But I can give you some few additional facts of a personal nature which will, I think, help to make the position clearer.

To begin with, then, I experienced two kinds of Orthodoxy when I was incarnate. I was a priest of two denominations—successively, I need hardly add! In the first, I had my upbringing, and into that I was ordained priest. After some years I felt dissatisfied with it.

On so many occasions I was called upon to decide too many questions of religious moment solely by my own powers of thought and reason. I had to do my own thinking upon matters which I felt the Church of which I was a member should have already made its own decisions and pronouncements. It was Authority which I felt was lacking; Authority upon vital questions and problems regarding the soul and the life to come.

This Church boasted no authoritative voice, could point to nothing better nor more secure than the *opinions* of churchmen generally. Eventually, I turned to that religious organisation which not only claimed for itself the voice of authority, but also spoke with a sure and certain voice—so I then imagined—and, moreover, claimed that that voice was infallible in its teachings. In this Church there was no need to think for one's self. The thinking had already been done by others properly equipped for the work so that all the 'faithful' were required to do was to follow the Church's teachings and obey its laws.

Into this second denomination I was 'received', and as it did not—and does not—recognise the validity of the clerical orders of the Church from which I had just seceded, I was re-ordained priest. I remained a member of this body until I passed into the spirit world at my dissolution.

So you will see, I have had some experience of

Orthodoxy of two kinds, the one fairly free and easy-going, the other rigorous and unremitting. The first permitting private judgement upon most religious matters; the second allowing only the voice of authority to speak.

But suppose, one of my friends might say, suppose one were to sweep away all the established forms of religion which are comprehended under the appellation of Orthodoxy and to which I take such objection, what would one put in its place? Assuredly there must be some kind of moral code. Christianity has stood the test of time, and the soul naturally yearns for some sort of religious expression, even if it be only of the simplest description, such as the Christian religions spread throughout the earth so amply afford its many members.

People have always leaned towards some form of public worship, though, in good truth, the congregations of them seem to be dwindling, but that is only because a certain vigour is perhaps temporarily lacking, and because folk are mentally tired after passing through such dreadful travail as the earth has undergone. So, again, what would you put in the place of Christian Orthodoxy?

The answer is simple, my good friend. Just this: the *Truth*.

Let us consider the position of affairs as they are upon earth at this moment of earthly time. By affairs, I mean principally 'religious' affairs; things that concern the very substance of what religion ought to be on earth, but which it most emphatically is not.

From the point of view of every individual who lives a number of years of his life upon earth, who then 'dies' and departs for some mysterious and awful destination in some vague unseen world—to heaven or to hell—from the viewpoint of such a person the situation is much the same now as it was hundreds of years ago.

The traditional teachings of Orthodoxy have seen to that. Most people on earth are thinking upon the same lines about 'death and the afterlife' as they were thinking two thousand years ago, and feeling much the same about it, too. That feeling in most cases is one of fear; fear of death itself and fear of the unknown and (as some would aver) unknowable future.

Before we proceed further, I would like to make one observation. During the course of these present writings I may find it necessary to repeat some statement that I have already made in my earlier discussions with you. I do so solely with the object of making myself as clear as possible. If my good friends will therefore bear with me in this, I, for my part, will promise to make such reiterations brief!

I could, of course, refer my readers to such previous writings by name, but that, I am persuaded, would be far more tedious and irritating to them than the plain but passing repetition of some particular fact or feature.

To resume. It has been remarked that some words reputed to have been spoken by Jesus and set down in the Gospels have had the effect of changing the whole course of history. The words to which I refer are those which he addressed, according to the printed text, to one of his disciples, namely, these: *Thou art Peter, and upon this rock I will build my church; and the gates of hell shall not prevail against it.*

The Church of which I was a member at the time of my dissolution claims this particular text as practically the foundation upon which the whole structure of the Church rests. That Jesus never gave voice to such an astonishing utterance is a matter of common knowledge to millions of us here in these realms of the spirit world. When I was on earth these very words gave me a feeling of the greatest security possible, for here I perceived, as

I thought, the very mandate for extravagant claims put forward by the Church.

The statement as it appears in the printed copies of the New Testament is nothing but a deliberate interpolation, a complete fabrication, and a mischievous one. And that is not the only interpolation. There are many others of a similar character, inserted with similar intentions, namely, that of buttressing up a system of religious authority. The Scriptures have not suffered from interpolations alone, for what is equally bad, so much has either not been recorded or has been deliberately deleted. By careful deleting and careful interpolating, certain real truths have been effectively suppressed.

What was the real and full purpose of the life of Jesus of Nazareth upon earth? The Churches throughout the earth are mostly in agreement in their answer to this question, and it would be to this effect: That God sent His only-begotten son to redeem the world from its sins, and by his death and resurrection he demonstrated his victory over the grave. The downfall of Adam and Eve cast the stain of original sin upon all mankind, and nothing would appease the wrath of God but that his 'only son' should offer himself as a sacrifice and die a shameful death. That in a few words is the sum of Christian faith.

It is because that statement is such an *appalling* untruth—indeed, it contains *not one* syllable of truth in it—that I feel so strongly upon the subject of Christian Orthodox teachings. The fact that I upheld such teachings when I was incarnate rather intensifies my present attitude. What I taught upon earth, both as preacher and spiritual advisor, I taught because I believed it to be the truth.

I know now that it was not and is not the truth. It may be objected that there must be millions who are, or were, similarly situated to myself. That is so; there are millions more like me. But it has been my great good fortune, by a somewhat long concatenation of circumstances, to have the opportunity to make return visits to earth, to speak through an old friend and recount some of my experiences, and thus try to off-set the dissemination of religious untruths for which I was responsible when I was on earth.

You will recall that I had something of a large public following both as preacher and writer, and thus caught both the ear and eye of a great number of people. I claim no privilege in what I am doing now. There have been many others before me; there will be many others to come after me. I shall retain my anonymity. It is what I say that matters, not who I am nor who I was.

It is nigh upon two thousand years since he who is called the 'Founder of Christianity' trod his way upon earth. And this is perfectly clear: it was never his intention to found a Church upon earth—nor elsewhere. Indeed, he was not the least interested in any new religion.

He was concerned with the truth. He came not to demonstrate any 'victory' over death. Death is not an opponent or an enemy; it is a natural process, the operation of a natural law which has been so functioning for aeons of time before the advent of Jesus. He had no need to 'fight' death. It cannot be fought in the sense of overcoming some malign influence.

Certain it is that in some cases of illness dissolution can be postponed by the exercise of the mind. A cheerful mind can work wonders in the case of some illnesses and so help towards a recovery where, on the contrary, a doleful, pessimistic temperament would hinder natural forces in their work of healing the physical body. In any case, it is but a postponement of dissolution, for dissolution is bound to come either sooner or later.

Jesus, therefore, could not, and would not, and did not, claim that he had gained any 'victory' whatsoever by his transition. What he did prove beyond any vestige of doubt is the fact of human survival of death of the physical body, and he proved this by the same means as thousands of other people have used both before and since his time he went back to earth and spoke to his friends there, showed himself, showed that he lived, and that death concerned the physical body only.

What of the teachings that Jesus gave to the remote corner of the earth where he lived? Orthodoxy has made havoc of the truth. The New Testament, wherein are alleged to be some of the acts and sayings of Jesus, has undergone all manner of accident from interpolations, omissions, deletions, mistranslations, mis-statements, and mis-interpretations. Even as the books stand at this present day they represent but a sorry fragment of all that Jesus said and did. As it is now the New Testament is one of the most dangerous of books since by its incompleteness it can so easily be mis-read.

How many Christian religions are there in existence upon earth this very day? There are literally *hundreds,* and most of them are based upon wide variations of scriptural interpretations of some one text or another. Each of these religious bodies is in varying degrees of conflict or disagreement with the others; each claiming to be right in itself, and one, at least, claiming to be the one true Church from which all the other major establishments have separated or otherwise found their origin.

However much these various and varying bodies may disagree among themselves, they all have one feature in common—monumental error. The error, broadly speaking, consists in regarding the *Christian* religion and all that it connotes as the standard, the very summit, of all religious thought in the universe. The Christian religion then towers high above all other forms of spiritual thought and ideas, and is even extended to 'heaven', which is essentially Christian.

The remainder will no doubt be looked after adequately enough in the 'life to come', but the Christian will ever and always come first in the heavenly scheme of things. Now this is no exaggeration, for such ideas have been existing on earth for nearly two millenniums, to become intensified as time passed on.

Thou art Peter, and upon this rock I will build my Church. A Church has most certainly been built. And how has Christianity shown itself during its passage through the years? Badly enough. Bethink you of the masses of extraordinary dogma and doctrines that have been invented, the incomprehensible creeds that have been fashioned, the strange rites and ceremonies that have been introduced into the religions of the earth.

Bethink you, too, of the presumption, the gross presumption, of the leaders of religious sects and denominations who pretend to know so much of God's purposes, His wishes, His will, His intentions, His reasons, and who have presented to the earth world such a terrible, inhuman and unhuman spectacle of the God of their fashioning and fabrication.

Recall, also, how they have instilled fear into the hearts of so many countless millions of good estimable folk during the ages past, the fear for their spiritual lives, with threats of dire punishment from a wrathful God, of everlasting burnings in eternal hell fires for the 'unrepentant'. Remember, also, the massacres and butcheries that took place in other times in the name of Christianity.

Regard the intolerance of religious might, how one faction would revenge itself upon another as soon as it came to power, each producing its 'martyrs' for the 'faith'. The pages of the history book of the Christian religion are blood-stained, and the text tells of terrible and ghastly deeds done in the name of its founder, and not only of its founder, but even in the name of God Himself.

Orthodox religion of one sort or another is a mass of complexities and spiritual pit-falls, and the state of a person's well-being in the spirit world is made dependant upon the most absurd man-made trivialities purporting to be founded upon the teachings of Jesus.

But what is all this?—I hear some friend say; surely you are putting yourself into something of a passion over very little. After all, this is ancient history you are talking about, and we have done with that kind of thing on earth now. We do not have religious persecutions any more. People are allowed to choose their own religion and worship God after their own fashion. This is the age of religious liberty.

That is perfectly true. It is history that I am recounting to you, and very unwholesome history, too. It is equally true that religious martyrs are not made in these times, martyrs, that is, to the extent of giving up their earthly lives. But you must remember that the vast concourse of people who suffered under the flail of Orthodoxy in the past ages are *all still alive* and resident in the spirit world. They are perfectly happy now, of course, but they are living witnesses to the pernicious nature of the whole system and its fallacious teachings.

There may be no persecutions upon religious grounds, but spiritual blindness still afflicts humanity upon earth. The number of those who are better informed and more enlightened upon such matters is infinitesimal by comparison with those who are still ignorant of spiritual *truths* as opposed to the spurious teachings of the Churches. They represent but a drop in a vast ocean of spiritual ignorance.

I have not really put myself into a passion, but so many of us in these realms are keenly sensitive of the unhappy state in which so many folk arrive in these lands at their dissolution, an unhappiness that is so often caused by the way they have been taught from their churches while they were incarnate.

As you will know, part of my work consists, with others, in helping people when they are making their advent into spirit lands so that my companions and I speak not only from experience but with feelings of exasperation that the tide of humanity still flows into these lands bringing with it all the Orthodox ignorance and lack of spiritual knowledge which it has gathered during the earthly passage.

You can well imagine our joy, indeed, heart-felt jubilation, when we go to meet some soul who has knowledge of the spirit world, of its truths and laws, and has practised communication with other folk in these realms. Never is our work so easy and so felicitous as upon such occasions. Most important of all, never is transition so pleasant for the principal person concerned than when all these conditions prevail. Indeed, there is very little for us to do actively in such cases. We merely rejoice with our new friend. Such instances are almost a holiday for us! But the picture has a reverse side, and an unpleasant one.

We spoke of religious liberty just a moment ago. Where literally is that freedom? A man, you will say, is permitted to worship where and when and in what manner he pleases. That also means he is at liberty to absorb into his mind all the travesties and distortions of truth and all the fallacious doctrines of a multiplicity of different religious denominations, such as are amply displayed throughout the earth world.

He is also at liberty to find the truth, but, alas, he will seldom or never find it in the very places wherein it should be preached and taught—the Churches. (I would, of course, hasten to except those courageous clergymen who, possessing the knowledge, have no fear of telling the truth about the spirit world from their pulpits. Unhappily such men are few, but any congregation of people should consider itself triply blessed in having a minister of such enlightenment to speak spiritual *truths* to it).

For two millenniums the Christian world has been living in spiritual blindness. Again I hear you say, perhaps, that I am exaggerating things too much. I am not, but I would ask you to view the situation from our point of view. Place yourselves in our position, as residents of the spirit world, and you will see not that I am overstating, but that I am understating.

You who are still incarnate do not see the results of spiritual ignorance and the lack of knowledge of conditions of life here that are bound to come to every soul after he leaves the earth plane for permanent residence in the spirit world.

Spiritual lethargy seems to enfold so many folk on earth; they drift along 'worshipping' according to the prayer-book, reciting creeds that have not one fraction of sense in them, and would be useless in any case, for theological creeds have no spiritual value; saying prayers which have little purport and less effect; placing their 'faith' in a hundred and one bizarre beliefs; content to base their future spiritual security upon the most trivial of superstitious practices; willing to be witnesses of, and partakers in, elaborate ritualistic displays, the symbology and purpose of which is mostly of no value whatever to a person's spiritual welfare.

Such folk have been stuffed for years with grotesque

ideas, oft-times monstrous ideas, upon the attributes of the Father of the Universe. God, to them, is a Being to be feared and loved and adored—thus they have been taught by blind 'authority'; a Being from whom, as a last hope, one can plead for mercy for the 'sins' one has committed while upon earth. Such people have had it dinned into their ears—and into the ears of their fathers before them—that man is a 'miserable sinner'. Does not almost every prayer in the printed books of them contain some such grovelling admission? A God of wrath!

While extremely vague, tenuous, unsubstantial prospects are held out to those who placate the Church's capricious God, theologians do not seem to have any doubts of what will befall if a man misbehaves himself upon earth. The rewards seem few and uncertain, but the punishments are many and decided. So mankind, if he thinks at all, will spend his lifetime on earth in fear not only of death itself, but of what is to happen to him after death has come at last.

What is the chief prospect according to the word of theological authority? *Judgement!*—with no chance of regaining lost spiritual ground. Judgement—without appeal. There is, however, some expectation of this 'justice' being tempered with mildness so that the only real hope at that 'last awful dread day'—such are the obnoxious terms employed by stupid theologians—is mercy.

What primitive, barbaric conceptions! Two thousand years of Christian Orthodoxy can teach nothing better, nothing nearer the truth, than that. The religious teachers, firmly believing all this most mischievous nonsense and arrogantly teaching it to the 'faithful', are directly responsible for allowing myriads of their deluded people to pass into the spirit world not only with profound ignorance upon them of the true state of things in these lands, but deceived by a tissue of erroneous teachings which have to be corrected before the newly arrived soul can take up his life, his undoubted heritage, in these peerless lands.

You will readily recall what I have told you about the dreadful fears which overwhelm so many souls upon their arrival here, fears for their very lives. There are no fears to be experienced upon earth that are remotely akin to them. Many folk are terrified of dissolution; they fear the actual process itself may be painful. They may pass over to us here with those fears somewhat diminished by their discovery that it is not painful, albeit there may be some prior condition of physical distress and pain, according to the cause of the transition.

But the transition itself is painless. After they have gone through this seeming ordeal and found that they are and feel very much alive, then comes the crushing thought of what they have been taught on earth to expect—*judgement*. (Whether they are to undergo that judgement then and there, or at some future date, they know not, of course, but the very uncertainty adds to their fears.) That is far worse than all the presumed terrors of death, for here, seemingly, they have reached the last barrier of everything, perhaps life itself.

They feel themselves securely enclosed within a trap from which there is no possibility of escape. Faced with what they believe to be hopelessly inevitable, they are sickened with such overwhelming dread as to paralyse their very powers of thought. Again I would say: do not imagine that I am exaggerating the state of affairs for I assure you that I am not. We, who are actively engaged in helping folk in such moments of dire distress, are surely the best judges of that, and there are many, many of my colleagues and companions who would feelingly endorse and corroborate what I am telling you.

Fear, my good friends, is what dominates the lives of most people who spare a minute to think upon their possible or probable state of existence in the spirit world, and that fear is carried with them when they come to dwell here for all time. Why should people have this fear? Whence is it derived? The answer is a plain one: it is years and years of Orthodox teachings that alone are responsible.

Do you wonder, then, that we speak feelingly, and perhaps with some little warmth at times, when we are continuously the witnesses of the pernicious results of these long years of religious errors. The Churches for the most part exist in a condition of spiritual darkness, not the darkness of deliberate evil, but the gloom of ignorance, and they are content to remain so, and keep their 'faithful' with them. It is we in the spirit world who have to rectify all their monstrous errors and remove the unwarrantable fears which they have cast upon the minds of so many of the earth's millions.

Miracles

It has been aptly remarked that a man is at the mercy of his biographer, to which it might be added, as a natural corollary, that he is also at the mercy of its readers, and any subsequent biographers. The strict duty of such a functionary is to record facts which are fully authenticated, and whatever are only opinions should be clearly stated to be such.

It is when the writer begins to draw upon his own imagination and ascribe motives for which there is no substantiation that the trouble begins. I can speak from experience in this because my own biographers have erred in this respect. They sometimes profess to know my character so well, and their appraisement has been reached more by supposition and inference than by direct reference to absolute knowledge. In extenuation, though, it must be said that it is almost impossible to know a person really well while he is still incarnate, so that in such instances there is much to be forgiven the writers.

If these inaccuracies can occur in the writing of a biography of an unimportant person on earth, how is the life of Jesus affected, the most famous of all biographies, for so in part it can be styled?

Now I know what some of my friends will say at once: Why, such a book cannot be compared, even remotely, with any other upon earth. The New Testament is an inspired work, inspired moreover, by none other than God Himself. Whatever appears in it, therefore, must be the truth.

If that were really so, then there would be nothing more for me to say, but it is not so. The New Testament is not inspired by God. A primary acquaintance with a few of the laws of the spirit world will easily and quickly demonstrate that.

Among the early revelations which come to ministers of the Church of whatever denomination when they come to live in these lands are the revelations by which, through their very life here, they are enabled to assess the New Testament at its true evaluation. Students of this book always find an ample field for investigation, comparison, and even for pungent comment.

Never did a biography labour under such a terrible handicap as does that which contains the life of Jesus, and that handicap might be described as a tragic and lamentable misconception. It is so disastrous a misconception, in fact, as to throw the whole character of the book into a realm where no other person has penetrated, or ever will penetrate.

It makes so much appear possible, where, in point of fact, so many things are impossible—the raising of the 'dead', to give one example from many. To come to the point, this gigantic misconception is none other than the *deifying* of Jesus. Whatever is normally inexplicable becomes nominally explicable by the simple statement that Jesus was himself God made man. In that capacity he can perform 'miracles', and that he must have performed many more than are recorded is the general opinion of incarnate man.

At the very outset the circumstances accompanying the birth of Jesus on earth were not normal. Theology claims for him a nativity that is anything but the outcome of a natural process. Orthodoxy is divided upon this question. Some say that his birth was in no manner different from that of any ordinary person, while others aver that his mother gave him life through the power of the Holy Spirit.

The latter is what I believed when I was on earth. Even the mother of Jesus is made to be an exception to the doctrine of original sin. She, it seems, was born without the stain that was cast upon all mankind by the sin of our supposed first parents, Adam and Eve. That, of course, has no confirmation from the Scriptures. It is just a pious invention of later times.

The story of the first Christmas on earth is a picturesque one as one reads it in the Gospels, provided too much thought is not brought to bear upon the narrative in view of the primitive nature of the times and circumstances. Since that first event, the earth has seen the rise of an immense number of pleasant customs and legends connected with its annual celebration. As a festival it has always been a homely one, since it dealt so largely with a process common to all humanity, and without which there would be no human being upon earth. Birthdays are regarded as pleasant memorials, and the birth of Jesus was an event in which all Christendom could share.

When Christmas-time approaches on earth we are very conscious of it in the spirit world for many thoughts reach us here in pleasurable anticipation of the coming festivities. It is, indeed, the only season of the earthly year when a surge of kindliness leaves the earth, to rise, as it were, into the spirit world. We in these lands have no interest in Christmas as an ecclesiastical feast, but we are profoundly overjoyed because of the many minds which give us some remembrance at that time, even though they may forget us for the rest of the year!

The story of the birth of Jesus on earth, as narrated in the New Testament, brings us immediately into a realm of mysteries and marvels, as well as 'supernatural' events. The angelic prophecy given to the shepherds, with its rapid fulfilment, and later the visit of certain wise men who were led by the 'supernatural' movement of a star to that part of the earth where Jesus was born, and the rest, taken together, constitute a delightful story, a story which has captured the fancy of man on earth and made the name and tide of Christmas synonymous with all that is kindly and ideally pleasant; a joyous, happy time.

As such it is to be forever commended for its sterling worth as a means of spiritual resuscitation of man upon earth. But the same story, taken in conjunction with the whole narrative of the life of Jesus, is one in which the truth has been obscured. That Jesus was born into the earth world is a truth beyond cavil or doubt, but that there was no 'miracle' attached to either his birth or the accompanying events is also a truth.

The word miracle, of course, is one that is frequently attached to numerous events scattered throughout the four Gospels. Those miracles are stated to have been performed by Jesus, and they are claimed by the Church, or some sections of it, as proving the divinity of Jesus. The so-called miracle of his birth, of course, stands by itself.

What precisely is a miracle, or rather, how would one define the term? According to earthly language, a miracle is the occurrence or performance of some wonderful event or act by Supernatural means or agency. That introduces another word which requires elucidation. Supernatural would be defined, I think, as being above the forces of nature, or beyond the realm of natural laws. *That is an utter impossibility.*

The laws of nature are pre-eminent. What appears to be a 'miracle' is not so at all. It is solely the employment of natural forces according to natural laws. The whole functioning of the spirit world is based upon natural laws. No one, either in these realms in which I live, or in any realms higher or lower in spiritual status, can move one fraction of an inch beyond any spiritual law. The seeming miracles which Jesus is reputed to have performed are in reality, therefore, not miracles at all, in the generally accepted sense of the term, but the utilising of natural forces.

If those particular acts of Jesus which are denominated miracles are regarded as acts performed by Jesus as God made man, then such acts can have little or no meaning for humanity in this present year of your earthly time. They are local and contemporary; local to the region where Jesus himself lived, and contemporary with his times. They were of inestimable service to those concerned, healing the sick, curing the blind, 'raising the dead to life'—of which I shall have something to say to you later on—and the many other deeds of noble service to suffering humanity. They are a record, though but a scanty one, of outstanding achievements. Many a tormented soul must have earnestly wished that Jesus lived upon earth at this day to bring aid in similar fashion.

Thus regarded, such acts are merely incidents of which to read in the New Testament. In a word, they have no practical application to life as it is lived on earth at this present time.

But to the psychic student these acts of Jesus present a very different picture. They cease to be local and contemporary, and they become a record, lacking in anything like voluminous detail, it is true, but a valuable record, nevertheless, of the 'power of the spirit', of the use of natural forces through a human instrument trained to absolute perfection in the exercise of psychic abilities.

These abilities are resident within every human being. In some they lie fallow, and so remain: in others they are dormant, but are developed eventually and employed in the service of fellowman. The number of such people is lamentably small by comparison with the earth's millions. But they do exist, as they have existed on earth from the earliest times.

It was never part of the scheme of things that our two worlds, yours and ours, should be separated, as it were, into two compartments forever shut off from each other from sight and sound. The means have always existed whereby the people of the world in which I live could communicate with the people of the world in which you live. But Orthodoxy, in one form or another, has tried to eliminate spiritual intercourse, or to prevent it, by suppressing the instruments whereby such communication is effected. Orthodoxy was not successful—and never will be. The spirit world is vastly stronger than Orthodoxy, and will ever be so.

Now it should be emphasised at once that these psychic abilities are perfectly natural things. They are inherent in every human being born upon earth. Through long years of disuse they have not atrophied; they are still there, but they are dormant and therefore need 'bringing out' by proper development. At the present time the possession of such abilities may be regarded as decidedly 'queer' by some folk, and the possessors of them as people who are really not quite 'right'—'peculiar' people, in fact! Both the psychic faculties and the owners of them are anything but normal. Such an appraisement is utterly wrong.

How often does one hear on earth the question: why is it necessary for me to go to a *medium*—for so are the possessors of these faculties designated—in order to speak with my friends who have passed on?

There would be no need whatever to go elsewhere for what such people seek if they would but do what is palpably obvious, namely, develop their own psychic powers and exercise them in the manner in which they were *intended to be exercised.*

Certain feelings of distaste will perhaps arise in the minds of some that they may be 'tapping' forces which are decidedly better left alone; some again will say that the indulgence in such practices as speaking to the 'departed' both unnatural and unhealthy, unhealthy physically, and most decidedly unhealthy spiritually. To all of which I would say peremptorily: Nonsense!

Man upon earth has no realisation of his own inherent powers. His earthly life is bounded solely by his five senses. He takes no heed or has no knowledge of his psychic senses which, under proper development, are capable of being brought to the surface, as it were, and used just as easily as the physical senses. There are, of course, people who, with acute religious sensitivity, object that it is not right and proper thus to 'disturb the dead', and that, in any case, one is not meant to know anything about these things because God does not wish it so.

In times past, the same senseless objections were raised when any new and revolutionary invention was brought before the people of earth. There were often loud cries that such innovations were against Holy Writ, as though Holy Writ contained *all* that was spiritually necessary for mankind on earth. Holy Writ is but one tiny and rather ill-formed drop in a colossal ocean of spiritual knowledge.

It is perilous to suppose that Holy Writ is the last word upon matters which concern man's conduct upon earth. Yet the Church, or at least one section of it, teaches just that. When I lived on earth I believed that all revelation between God and man had ceased, and that with the passing of the last of the Apostles no further word from God would be sent to earth.

If I may, I would like to digress for a moment—a habit to which my friends are surely becoming accustomed! Since I have lived in the spirit world, I have many times contemplated upon the extraordinary beliefs which I held and propagated when I was a priest of the Church. Of course, I am not alone in this; experience with my many friends has shown me that there is hardly a minister of the Church, except those fortunate men who were spiritually enlightened before they came to spirit lands, who at some time does not think deeply upon the beliefs he held when incarnate, the reliance which he placed upon what have since revealed themselves as sheer trivialities, together with the strange things he preached from his pulpit as spiritual truths.

What a narrow little world we worked in! We tried, as it were, to confine this gigantic, superbly organised and transcendingly beautiful spirit world within a few words taken from an ancient book. We tried to make entry into this wonderful world dependent upon some childish rule based upon a text extracted from that same ancient book: or conditional upon obedience to some manufactured rule of the Church.

What right had I, so I have often thought, to proclaim the law of God upon this or that; to make entry into these or other realms of the spirit world possible only upon submission to some 'commandment' of the Church? For what I did, I can only claim spiritual blindness, and hasten to speak the truth as I know it now. During those days on earth I never dreamed that one simple text from that very book, upon which so many people place such complete reliance, literally held the clue to the whole of life on earth as it is concerned with the life in these lands.

Whatever a man sows upon earth that will he reap in the spirit world. Such is a full statement of the text. That is the law. The great, inescapable, inevitable, infallible law of cause and effect. It is minutely exact and perfect in its operation. It is incorruptible; there is no bribery that will touch it; no privilege can lodge a claim against it. It operates alike upon all men, regardless of age or sex, regardless of social position; regardless of occupation. Whether 'king or commoner', cleric or layman, rich or poor, *all* come *alike* under the supreme law of cause and effect, and it acts in exactly the same manner with each individual.

There is no deviation, or variation. It is constant and invariable, precise and exact. It cannot be tampered with; it cannot be evaded through the supposed offices of another person of whatever spiritual status. It is unremitting and unrelenting. It permits the exercise of no mercy. It is frigidly just. Indeed, it is justice itself. It needs no administration. It administers itself, truly, absolutely, and irrevocably. The whole is comprehended in that one brief text: *Whatsoever a man soweth, that also shall he reap.*

On many, many occasions did I see those words, but never did I realise their true meaning—just as I have this minute given it to you. Could any law be more perfect? Assuredly not, for in that law rests the certainty of spiritual progression for all mankind. There is no talk here of Judgement and Judgement Days, no word here of eternal damnation. No word of an avenging God inflicting dreadful punishments upon a man because he has sinned against Him. It is just a plain statement of fact.

However bad may be the harvest that is reaped by

each individual as a consequence of the life he has led upon earth, he has the whole of eternity before him during which to sow well, and reap the richest of rich harvests. It may take time and great effort; it may cost the individual much mental anguish; there may be overwhelming remorse; but the soul will have, and does have, every aid and opportunity to regain whatever ground he has lost, and so rise to the greatest heights in spiritual advancement.

No effort is ever wasted. No trivialities of strange doctrines nor church 'commandments' will obtrude to impose frivolous conditions upon our progressional endeavours. We are the owners of our own soul, free by immutable right to help ourselves out of the spiritual morass into which our mode of living on earth has cast us; we all have the illimitable resources of the spirit world to aid us at our smallest cry.

It requires no elaborate ritual or ceremonial, but just our own concentrated and determined efforts to retrieve our lost ground. Progression is *free and open* for every soul that has been, is being, and will be, born upon earth. No Church or other organisation whatever can interfere with, or hinder or obstruct, the operation of that law. No mandate has been given to any Church or other religious institution by which it can deem itself the sole means of gaining entrance to these or any other realms of the spirit world.

Man alone decides what part or region of the spirit world shall be his initial destination when he quits the earth-plane at his dissolution. His mode of life upon earth has decided that, but his mode of life does not include the obeying of some purely ecclesiastical law imposed by ecclesiastical authorities upon all adherents to its particular brand of religious 'faith'.

Forced attendance at certain church services upon

pain of eternal damnation in default thereof is a glaring example of gross spiritual presumption. As a spiritual law it is utterly and completely ineffective, but it is none the less mischievous since it inspires fear within the mind of many an otherwise unoffending individual, and is totally opposed to the truth of the life and laws of the spirit world.

The Church, in fact, presumes to *judge* upon a man's spiritual condition by laws of its own fabrication, and does so in the name of God, claiming that such laws are God's laws. What does the Church know of God's laws? Or to put it another way: what does the Church—any Church *know* of the laws of the spirit world, the natural laws which govern these lands and govern our lives here?

What does the Church know, for example, of the natural law of cause and effect, for that is one of the Father's laws? The answer is that the Church knows *nothing whatever,* guesses a great deal—and wrongly and presumes to know so much. And the Church has assumed to itself the care of men's souls on earth. What a preposterous state of affairs concerning matters that are so vital, so urgent, of such supreme importance.

Well, now, these are just some few of the thoughts that have passed through my mind from time to time since my coming to live in these lands. Some such thoughts occur to so many of the clergy when they come to dwell here.

This has been a long digression, but I am persuaded that you will not be displeased with me for breaking in upon what I was saying by setting down these thoughts for your contemplation. As a priest who abided by a rigidly narrow creed and urged others to join with him, as I was bound to do, I discovered when I entered these beautiful realms of the spirit world that it was not the influence of religious 'faith' which had brought me here, nor any adherence to ecclesiastical laws or 'commandments', but something much deeper, and sounder, and safer—indeed, the only *safe* thing, namely, the *kind* of life I had led while I was incarnate.

Now let us resume. The so-called miracles of Jesus, I have tried to explain to you, were in truth no miracles at all, but solely the exercise of his superlative psychic faculties. Such faculties as are to be found on earth at this very moment of time. But there is this difference. Jesus had spent long years in training and developing those faculties, and he combined within the one individual *all* the psychic gifts it is possible to possess, and they were developed to the *highest possible degree*. Thus he is unique among men.

But he was not, and he is not, God. Potentially, *every human being born upon earth could do precisely what Jesus did*. That is a statement which I want to emphasise. The fact that no one has done so in no way contradicts that truth. It is man's own fault that he does not utilise his potentialities. Certainly, it would make heavy inroads upon his patience and time and endurance to attain merely half the psychic skill that Jesus was able to acquire, apart altogether from *spiritual* development.

In the world of music on earth you have your great instrumental virtuosi. Their names are 'household words'. Why should not the realm of psychic faculties also have its virtuosi? Jesus himself was one. He devoted himself—just as the famous instrumentalist does—to years and years of study. He perfected his technique—to continue in our use of musical idiom, since the cases are exactly parallel both in kind and condition—and when he finally emerged before the public he came to serve, his performance was as flawless as it was spiritually and humanly possible to be.

At least one famous violinist was accused of being in league with 'the devil' because of his amazing prestidigitation upon his instrument. It was manifestly impossible, so some of his auditors exclaimed, that a man unaided by 'the devil' could ever perform such feats of manual dexterity upon any instrument. They did not go so far as to call it a 'miracle'. In this case it was just Satan at work.

With Jesus it was slightly different. His supreme gifts were called 'miracles' on the one hand and attributed to Satan upon the other! The satanic theory is merely laughed at in these days, but the 'miracle' theory still persists. For any person to emulate Jesus in the high degree of perfection of his psychic capacities would require the existence of material circumstances, at the very outset, difficult of attainment. The conditions of life, generally, have so altered on earth, but that does not mean that no mediumship can be, or should be, developed at all.

Is there not a scriptural injunction that says *Try the spirits?* That there must be spirits is obvious, or else the words mean nothing. Assuming that there are such 'things' as spirits—and many people regard us as little more than mere 'things'—then how are they to be tested?

If they can be tested, then the natural conclusion is that they must make themselves known to incarnate man in some fashion or other. How? Through 'miracles' or other unusual 'supernatural' happenings? Hardly; for there would not seem to be enough of either to provide a sufficient field for investigation, beyond a few extremely flimsy instances alleged to have occurred within the Church. After all, a twentieth century 'miracle' rests upon such unsubstantial ground and is so rare (so you would be led to believe) that there is really no case to go upon. What then?

The only answer, and the right answer, as a great many folk have proved conclusively over and over again, is communication between the spirit world and the earth world. That is done by the use of psychic faculties, the same kind of faculties that Jesus himself used, the same kind of faculties whose exercise by him have been denominated 'miracles'.

Jesus was the great exemplar. He showed how man could live on earth, how man should *live* during his incarnate journey. He showed, too, how man should take cognisance of his full potentialities, and not restrict his earthly perceptions to his five senses alone. He clearly demonstrated how close are our two worlds, that the veil between them is, in truth, thin, and that it is not only possible but right that man on earth should be fully heedful of both worlds, the earth upon which he is temporarily sojourning and the spirit world, which will be his ultimate destination, and that being heedful of both, he can make his life a careful balance of the one and the other.

Jesus lived upon earth as a natural human being, eating and sleeping, and walking the countryside where he abided. But as he lived from day to day, his psychic faculties were always at the pitch of perfection, ready to be exercised upon the enormous number of occasions that presented themselves among a primitive people. He performed deeds that simple-minded people could not possibly explain. They seemed miraculous to some; to others it was obviously 'the devil'. At least the sick and the suffering could say in effect and in good truth: whether it be the devil or not, I am cured!

A strange devil, to say the least, that went about the land doing good!

Miracles Concluded

Of all the so-called miracles of Jesus none is more spectacular and sensational than that of 'raising the dead to life'. Here, it has been thought, is proof enough, if proof be wanting, that Jesus was God, for none other than God could perform such a stupendous act.

Before we go further it would be as well if, between us, we came to some conclusions as to the precise signification of the word 'dead'.

The word itself conveys a variety of meanings which are the outcome of a variety of theories. Let me put some of those meanings before you.

In the strict definition of the dictionary 'dead' means 'having ceased to live', or 'that from which life has departed'. As applying to the physical body after dissolution, that is an accurate statement enough. But some people will think in terms extending beyond that.

The 'dead', they will affirm, are not physical bodies from which life has departed. They are a class of beings, human beings presumably, and they are situated in some unseen locality in some unknown and unseen region, from which they do not emerge to return to the earth whence they departed—some would say because they cannot—and are therefore forever silent upon their condition and destination. Whether they have 'life' in them or not, or whether they are just sleeping, is not known for the same reasons.

In some cases the 'dead' are distinguished by the appellation 'holy souls'. Souls they most certainly are, but 'holy'—most certainly not. Incidentally, holy is not a word that is ever in favour in these realms. It savours too much of the sickly pious and the sanctimonious. It suggests invidious distinctions which are disliked profoundly. Both the words 'holy' and 'righteousness' are reminiscent of religious jargon, and as such are not in use here.

To return to our discussion of the 'dead'. There are other schools of thought who consider that the 'dead' are to be found in churchyards and cemeteries, or beneath the floors of churches and cathedrals which are used for the same purpose. In extreme cases it is literally believed that the bodies will rise up from their graves at the general resurrection, whenever that may be.

For the bodily disintegration which has taken place meanwhile doubtless adequate provision has been made under Providence—whatever that may mean. Proceeding still further, some folk would assert that whatever the 'dead' may be, or *wherever* they may be, they cannot be like us on earth. We who are on earth are *alive*, and as the earth is the natural habitat of human beings, everything is thus normal and as it should be. The *earth* is the standard of living places, not some speculative unseen regions, of which its 'heaven' may be the proper dwelling place for angels, and its 'hell' that of devils.

Those of our friends and relatives who have ceased to live on this planet are to be numbered among the 'dead'. And so on. Thus, you will perceive that the term 'the dead' can signify two things. It can refer to the corpses, or the remnants of corpses, which lie sepultured in graveyards in various stages of disintegration, and it can mean the souls, or the spirits, or the personalities of those same departed people. All of which is extremely confusing.

In speaking to you I have always used as precise terms as possible to avoid misunderstanding, and at the risk of prolixity introduced such phrases as 'During my earthly life,' or 'When I lived on earth,' or again 'When I was incarnate.' In this latter phrase I am speaking in earthly terms.

Incarnate simply means 'clothed in flesh', that is, 'in a physical body', if you prefer it that way. In thinking of me, doubtless you might do so under the term *disembodied,* meaning, of course, that I no longer have a physical body. Upon such a basis, I am persuaded, we should fully understand one another. But to be strictly accurate, that is, to speak with absolute truth, I can claim that I am unquestionably embodied, as I am from the point of view of the spirit world.

Moreover, that body is very much of a physical order to us. It is solid; it is natural; it is perfect in functioning and in general appearance; it is never ailing; it suffers from no fatigues, nor from hunger and thirst; It is imperishable, and it is in possession of its full complement of limbs, and so on. That is the body which houses me, whom you, my friend, as the reader, have come to know through these writings.

I am in no sense discarnate, but very much incarnate—as we all are in the spirit world. People on earth may regard me as 'dead', and that is something I vehemently repudiate, for I am very much alive! As applied to human beings, *there are no dead,* for all who have lived on earth are still living in the spirit world. They have never for one fraction of a moment ceased to do anything else but live.

Let us try, at least for our present purposes, to bring

some order into this confusion of terms, so that, in a moment or so when we come to talk about 'raising the dead to life', we may not precipitate ourselves into worse verbal difficulties.

Death applies to the physical body *only*. When a person dies, his physical body becomes inanimate. All life has been withdrawn from it, and it has to be disposed of in ways that are familiar enough to you. Disintegration will take place, quickly or slowly, according to circumstances and conditions, until eventually there will be very little left of the original physical frame that once trod the earth.

There is no possible way of restoring those remnants to their original state. No power on earth or from the spirit world can do that. It is an *absolute* impossibility. The belief that on the 'last day' dead bodies will rise up from their tombs is just plainly stupid. One moment's thought will show the absurdity of it. For one thing, it assumes that every human being is comfortably buried in a cemetery or other recognised burial-place, wholly ignoring the bodies of those other folk which by various means have become annihilated or totally consumed.

Orthodoxy has treated the physical body purely from the material standpoint, without any attempt being made to discover how the physical body is animated and what takes place upon dissolution. Had the subject had proper attention devoted to it, a full light would have been thrown upon the supposed miracle of 'raising the dead to life'.

The physical body is animated, is kept alive, by the soul of man—to put it at its simplest—which itself possesses a spirit body through which it functions and lives. The spirit body, with all its constituents, uses the physical body through which to manifest itself while upon its earthly sojourn. The two are securely, but not inseparably, joined together by a magnetic cord, a life line, so to speak, along which, as the current in an electric cable, there passes the force which provides *life* to the physical body.

It naturally does not provide full life to the physical body. Every incarnate person must obey certain laws by which the physical body is fed and otherwise cared for, and is, as it were, given its necessary fuel, as with a locomotive engine. Just so long as the magnetic cord is attached to the spirit body, then just so long will the physical body retain life in it. Just so long as the spirit body remains within the physical body, just so long will the physical body retain normal consciousness.

When ordinary sleep overtakes the physical body it is because the spirit body has temporarily withdrawn itself. The needs of the physical body include the necessity for a certain amount of sleep. It has to be recharged; the energy which has been consumed during the day's work has to be replaced. Though the amount of sleep required varies with individuals, some *sleep,* however small the quantity, is essential. This withdrawal of the spirit body during slumber is a natural process common to everyone, but what is more to our present purpose, the whole experience of sleep, regarded as a process, is closely akin to what is known to you upon earth as 'death'.

There is a difference, and, of course, you will say, a vital difference! It literally is vital, as far as the physical body is concerned. The difference, then, between sleep and 'death' is that in sleep the spirit body returns to its physical covering, and induces a return, or partial return, of physical consciousness, but at 'death' the spirit body relinquishes the physical body for ever. The magnetic cord becomes severed, the spirit of the individual, *the real person*, departs for its first self-appointed abode in the spirit world, while the physical body assumes all the unmistakable signs of its complete absence of animation, one of which is decomposition. No power, physical or spiritual, can revivify the corpse. It is dead, finally and completely.

The original owner of it has no further use for it. It is but a cast-off garment. But *he(*or *she)*is not dead; he is very much alive. He may be sleeping somewhere in these lands, for reasons which I have recounted to you on some previous occasions. But he is not 'resting in peace' according to the usual prayer-book understanding of that phrase. He is sleeping, and may be very much at peace, but it is a temporary sleep of remedial treatment, where such is necessary. The peace he will enjoy when he awakes will be the peace which the glories of the new life here will engender within him.

What an unimaginative notion that is which is embodied in the prayer, *Eternal rest give unto him, O Lord.* How thankful we all are here that this prayer is never answered! *Eternal rest!* I could really preach a most eloquent sermon upon those two words—if my days for sermons were not for ever ended! Many a clergyman has expressed similar sentiments to me.

What a wealth of glorious sermonic themes are discoverable in the truths of the spirit world. But the time has passed for that since we ourselves have passed into these lands. How many ministers of the Church have wished they could once again catch the ears of their former congregations, and tell them now a very different story. Were they able to do so in a wholesale fashion, how many of them would be believed? Up would rise the old familiar cry of 'the devil'.

So many churchmen find that by their preaching and teaching they have condemned to their congregations as being devilish the very things which they now find to be eternal truths. Thus, they have effectually closed the door in their own faces. There are exceptions, of course. With great good fortune, I am one of those exceptions. Little did I dream once upon a time that I should be able to return to the earth-plane to speak with those who still remember me. Concerning *eternal rest*, I shall chat to you later.

There is no need for me to recount to you the narrative of the occasions upon which Jesus 'raised the dead to life'. But there is this to be observed. The accounts themselves are sparing of details. It is safe to say that were such stories brought forward today in another context, they would never be given acceptance upon such scanty evidence. They are credited solely upon the basis that Jesus was himself God, and that the Scriptures wherein these accounts are set down are divinely inspired. The word of God, in fact.

In one instance Jesus is reputed to have brought to life a corpse which had been *entombed* for four days. So little hope was there that Jesus could do anything effective in the matter when he arrived upon the scene that one of the mourners is supposed to have drawn his attention to this fact by specific mention of the probability that 'by this time' the body of the deceased would be in a fairly advanced state of decomposition. The warmth of climate would doubtless be a contributive factor in this.

When Jesus was first approached for his help he made the remark, according to the Gospel, that the man's sickness 'was not unto death, but for the glory of God, that the Son of God might be glorified thereby.'

As the text stands you have an example of the work of interpolators. Jesus simply made a prognosis upon the case in hand. He merely stated that the man would not die of the sickness that was at present assailing him. That was all. Theologians ask you to believe that the man was allowed to fall into sickness for the express purpose that Jesus might manifest his authority and power, and glorify God by curing him.

Once again, it throws Jesus into a false position. What is infinitely worse, it suggests that God made people deliberately unwell, even allowed them to 'die'—an outrageous imputation. That Jesus was able to demonstrate the force of his psychic faculties is abundantly clear, but in so demonstrating them he was rendering a first service to his brothers on earth by healing the sick. It was not his work to go about performing alleged miracles as proof of his 'divine authority'. No man requires 'authority', divine or otherwise, to do good. Jesus did not prove he was God by what he did, but he proved what *could* be done with God's help, with right living, and by cultivating the psychic senses and faculties.

Jesus felt sufficiently assured that the man would not die because by his psychic senses he perceived the true situation of the case. His psychic prognosis was eventually proved to be wholly accurate. Though medical details are wanting in the account given, it is clear that the sick man had lapsed into a state of coma of sufficient depth to justify the verdict that he was 'dead'. Medical science being primitive in those days, who was to judge otherwise?

It is not surprising, then, to read that when Jesus eventually reached the man, it was to discover that he had been presumed 'dead', and accordingly buried. That Jesus was disturbed by this intelligence is natural, since entombing might have caused the man's transition, and so placed him beyond all reach of material aid whereas mere coma could be made to respond to treatment.

It did not take Jesus long to ascertain that he was not too late. He could see that the vital cord uniting the spirit body to the physical body was *still intact* Jesus gave his orders; he himself did what was necessary, and the supposedly 'dead' man was restored to his relatives. The psychic prognosis of Jesus was completely justified.

What applies in this particular case applies equally and positively in the other instances where Jesus 'raised the dead to life'. That the people concerned were most emphatically *not* 'dead', in the sense that their bodies were wholly without life, is simply a matter of spiritual truth. Had the physical bodies of these folk been inanimate, Jesus could not have restored them to animation.

Closely similar to these specific acts of Jesus are those which come under the designation of 'healing the sick'. Again, of course, Orthodoxy claims that Jesus was able to do so because he was himself God.

Throughout the Scripture text great emphasis is constantly laid upon 'faith' in connection with the many acts of healing. Jesus, on occasion, is reputed to have said to the sick person, *Thy faith hath made thee whole.* Theologians naturally make the most of such alleged utterances as these. The faith, some would say, means the belief that Jesus was God. Without this definite belief there would have been no cure. Or faith, others would declare, in the powers of Jesus as a healer of the sick. Whichever it may be, faith is essential.

How that brief word is overworked by churchmen generally. Believe this, or believe that, and you will be 'saved'.

Faith-healing, as it is termed, is practised on earth by some clergymen at this very day. They assemble the sick in their churches, and by the 'laying-on' of hands try to bring ease and comfort to the sick, and perhaps heal them altogether. Such methods are frowned upon in some quarters, in spite of the example set by their Master, but the use of the term 'faith-healing' helps to divert censure from an ecclesiastical superior.

Unless the patient has faith, they will say, they can do nothing. Healing the sick by spirit agency?—never! They would never be associated with such unclean things, they would assert with pious horror! This is purely a religious matter.

It would pay us to look a little closer into this question of healing by faith. In the first place, the word 'faith' lends itself to a variety of meanings, and consequently is applied in a variety of different ways and in different contexts.

Faith, says the old dictum, will move mountains. Here I boldly and emphatically assert that faith will do no such thing. Altogether *too much* is expected of faith. That is not the fault of faith, but of people's misuse of the word.

As far as faith-healing as practised by churchmen is concerned, faith is used to cover both their successes and their failures. If the patient is cured or receives obvious benefit, faith is the cause. If no success is achieved, then lack of faith is the reason. In either event the case for faith healing and all that it is supposed to connote is fully protected. Results, it would seem, rest with the patient. The clergyman will perhaps claim little for himself.

Thy faith hath made thee whole. Faith *alone* could do no such thing. If it is to make spiritual sense, that sentence should read 'Thy faith hath *helped* to make thee whole.' That is precisely all that faith can do. At most, faith—that is, the particular kind of faith we are now discussing—is a cheerful, optimistic state of mind, a hopeful attitude.

The faith that is reposed in a person or undertaking must be inspired. For example: if your own earthly doctor is a sound medical man, and your past experiences of his skill and abilities have proved his worth to you, you naturally and properly repose the utmost faith in any treatment which he may prescribe for you in your need.

If by chance he should fail to alleviate your trouble, whatever it may be, you will most probably still retain your trust in him, and regard the failure as perhaps a temporary one due to the obstinacy of your complaint. While personal recommendation may have taken you to him in the first instance, your subsequent *faith* in him is based upon evidence, and first-hand evidence, too. Your faith is something that is very lively and keen within you, if I may so express it.

You might find it difficult to describe the feeling in so many words, but the sensation of confidence is unmistakably there. So, it will remain, until a succession of failures to afford you relief should intervene to banish those feelings from your mind. That doctor will tell you that your optimistic and confident attitude towards his abilities as a physician and the treatment he is giving you will help enormously in bringing about a cure, if it is humanly and scientifically possible to effect a cure. But that attitude, by itself, would effect no result.

In this connection, then, faith, is best described as a hopeful, optimistic, even cheerful, state of mind, and not a blind belief.

Those among the clergy who practise faith healing or spiritual healing on earth are mostly wholly ignorant as to the means by which whatever successes they achieve are brought about. They would not claim miracles, but say that God, through the Holy Spirit and by their own imposition of hands, has, by His grace, brought about a cure, or relief, to the sick person.

Such cure or relief, they would assert, was only accorded by virtue of the faith of the person concerned. It is naturally presumed that the clergyman himself is possessed of some description of faith in what he is doing, otherwise he would be a party to what would be simply a mockery. Sincerity of purpose and an earnest desire to be of service to his fellow-men is the laudable motive behind such individuals. But these good fellows do not know what is taking place, nor how they attain whatever results they may have.

There are folk on earth who are in close communication and co-operation with us here, and who by the exercise of their psychic powers, are able to heal the sick. They are doing just such work as did Jesus when he was on earth, by the same means, and by the same power. They are mediums through which the power of the spirit world can be brought to bear upon the sick. Faith cannot produce a cure. It can help, and help widely, but of itself it is powerless to cure.

While the faith-healing minister in his church claims faith as the instrument of his curative work, in reality he does it solely by virtue of the fact that he is able to employ psychic faculties of which he is totally unaware. That he is unconscious of such powers makes no difference. Spirit power is at work, and he is the unknowing earthly agent of it. He may call it what he likes, but it makes no difference to the truth of the case.

What is the position on earth at this day of the healing of the sick by spirit action? Beyond those who are responsible for it and who are actively concerned With it, and those happy folk who know of, or enjoy, the great benefits of it, it is discredited, smiled at in a superior fashion, scoffed at, and generally ridiculed.

There are exceptions, naturally, to such a broad statement, but that is a fair estimate of the situation.

Yet those who are performing these *undoubted* acts of healing—undoubted, that is, by those who have been cured of their disabilities and by everyone else in close association with us of the spirit world—the healing mediums, are doing precisely what Jesus himself did. The witnesses for today's cures are living among you on earth, ready to attest to the truth of their cures and of my very words here.

Would Orthodoxy accept any such attestation? Does it even trouble to consider the subject at all? Here is evidence of spirit agency for churchmen to test, to carry out the scriptural injunction to *Try the spirits*. Have they done so? There is only one answer—to their eternal shame; *they have not*. They prefer to ignore the whole subject and the still greater truths which lie behind these splendid works of healing; they prefer to concentrate their thoughts and energies upon preaching from their pulpits about the 'miracles' of Jesus.

Completely misunderstanding, and so misinterpreting, the Scriptures wherein they read of the healing achievements of Jesus, they flatly discredit the whole scheme and providence of the spirit world; they are making the whole earthly dispensation, whereby man at all times and in all ages shall have at hand aid from the spirit world in his distress of body and mind, into an attenuated, privileged dispensation of roughly three years duration of earthly time—the three years, according to the Scriptures, during which Jesus performed his 'miracles'.

During the short span of three years—you are asked to believe—God Himself came upon earth as Jesus. He came to an obscure part of the earth, gave forth his teachings, most of which remain unrecorded, healed the sick, and so left the earth to return to the realms of heaven. And that was nigh upon two thousand years agone.

Have there been no sick people since that time? What of today, when there are so many broken and ailing bodies on your earth? Considered impartially, is not the need for Jesus and his powers greater *now,* at this present moment of time? Then why the extraordinary privilege granted to a small area of an eastern country so many long years ago?

It is useless to say, "It is God's will." Orthodoxy knows nothing of God's will. It is futile to say that you must not probe into the reasons for these things, but take them as they are. Divine Providence, the churchmen will declare, has not seen fit to send any measure of relief to earth through such another as Jesus. That is enough. The earth is steeped in sin; it is because of it that God has sent all the suffering that humanity has undergone recently, as a judgement upon its wickedness. Such is the magnificent voice of Orthodoxy.

Unfortunately for the earth world, Orthodoxy is two thousand years behind the times. It has lived in its narrow, restricted little theological world of creeds and dogmas and doctrines, blindly leading the blind deeper and deeper into the morass of spiritual ignorance. Theologians have transmogrified Jesus into a worker of 'miracles'. By their total misunderstanding of his faculties and powers they assert that he is God.

Upon this basis they set out to convert the 'heathen' and the 'savage' away from their false gods. The same heathen and savage was ready to deify anyone who could exhibit superior powers, and to worship him as his god. That is precisely what Orthodoxy has itself done. Failing dismally to perceive and recognise the true powers of Jesus and how and whence they were derived, how he used them, and why he used them, theologians have emulated the heathen, whom they regard as barbaric on account of his own deifications, and themselves deified Jesus.

They have raised him to the elevation of the Godhead, and completely obscured those very natural psychic faculties which he exercised for the benefit of his fellow-men. They have made him the performer of the most impossible feats, and the possessor of impossible attributes. They have accepted in a wholesale fashion an account which contains perhaps but half-a-dozen words concerning some act of Jesus, but refuse to accept the testimony of living witnesses upon earth, where full and complete evidence is there for their attention. It is the same power from the spirit world that is working upon earth at this moment of your time, and curing the sick.

The narrowness, self-satisfaction and stupidity of Orthodoxy is an eternal insult to the Father of the Universe. Churchmen have tried to encompass the Father within the restricted confines of their own small petty minds. They have tried to reduce His Wisdom to the puny dimensions of their own dull wits.

That is why in the spirit world there are so many churchmen and theologians, great and small, who have been compelled by force of the truth to change their views so radically that they now bear no resemblance to the views they held when incarnate. That is why my views have similarly changed!

Burial Service

During the course of some previous writings, I discussed with you certain aspects of the customary methods of disposing of the physical body after its 'death'.

Briefly, I told you how that all the religious ceremonials and mournful trappings which usually accompany the whole procedure of burial are in themselves bad; bad alike for the individual who has passed into these lands, and bad for those who are left behind upon earth.

Sorrow occasioned by the passing from earth of a cherished friend or relative is bound to exist as long as human affections themselves endure. That is but natural as things are at present. Ignorance or lack of knowledge of spiritual truths and of conditions of life in the spirit world will serve to intensify that sorrow.

This ignorance is not only upon the part of the individual; the Churches of most denominations share in it. It is to them, as supposed spiritual mentors, that the finger must be pointed for adding to the burden of sorrow which bereavement brings with it.

To perceive this ignorance of spiritual knowledge at its worst one needs but to examine the order of the Church's burial services. Here, indeed, is displayed ignorance of a monumental description. The so-called prayers of which these services are composed amply reveal just how out of touch are the Churches with spiritual realities. Instead of the prayers being a rich source of comfort to the mourners, and what is still more important, of sound practical help to the person who had 'died', they are, both to the former and the latter, utterly valueless.

Let us examine some of the prayers together, and you will see the force of my words. A large number of the prayers are simply biblical quotations, with generous extractions from the Psalms.

Here I must emphasise that what both the mourners and the 'departed' need is practical help. The mourner needs comfort in his trouble; the person who has just left the earth for all time needs assistance of a *material* kind. He may be in trouble of various sorts and degrees. He may require a great deal of purely spiritual help; he may want aid merely in the process of finding out what has taken place with him, where he is, what he is to do, how he is to do it, and a score of similar matters.

While we who are resident here do all we can upon this side, a direct appeal through prayer upon the part of the officiating minister will add to the power which is given to us in affording assistance to others. But they *must* be prayers of the right kind. Long quotations from some psalm or other, beautiful as they may be in their content and in their language, are wholly ineffective if those quotations have no bearing upon what is so urgently wanted, namely, direct assistance and guidance.

Here is another most important circumstance for which the Churches in their ignorance make no disposition. Burial services in the more temperate climes usually take place some days after the actual moment of passing.

The 'dead' person, in reality, has by then *passed and gone*. But it is at the actual moment of transition when the proper assistance can be of great value. I fully acknowledge that in every case it would not be possible to provide it then as circumstances of transition vary so widely.

But where the dissolution is about to take place with full warning of its imminence, that is the moment to send forth earnest prayers for help. Thus, you will see clearly that Church burial services, as they are at present constituted both as to time of performance and spiritual content, are mostly *too late* to be of any practical spiritual value to the departed person.

If then, you will recall these few remarks as we discuss the order of the burial service you will see plainly just how far is Orthodoxy removed from any knowledge of spiritual truths.

I should mention that under the designation burial service, I include all that takes place both in the Church and at the place of burial.

How many of the prayers are understood by the folk who are saying them, or supposed to be saying them? Words are framed into strange sentences which do not seem to have any application, direct or indirect, to the matter in hand, except in one way—they are guaranteed to make things infinitely worse for the mourners by the dismal and hopeless sentiments which they embody.

For a prayer to be successful, it must have force and direction behind it. A disinterested muttering and mumbling of some prayerful formula is of no earthly use whatever, nor of any heavenly use either. When, in addition, the words convey no possible meaning to the half-hearted reciter of them, an already bad case is rendered completely hopeless.

Prayers that incorporate appeals which are in direct

opposition to spiritual laws are similarly ineffective. Of what use to cry out against a natural law? Would anyone in his sane senses pray that the law of gravity might be suspended, or qualified in some way, or dispensed with altogether? In similar case are all those pleas for mercy for the departed one. You will recall what I have told you upon the subject of the 'mercy' of God.

Regarded as a whole, the principal theme running through the prayers of the burial services is that of uncertainty, of hopelessness almost. The Church is entirely in the dark regarding conditions of 'life after death'. It knows literally *nothing*. The prayers liberally reveal that ignorance.

I would ask you to keep well in mind what I have just mentioned to you concerning prayers for the departed person: how that they must be direct to the point by asking for help in clear terms, in terms, that is, which are fully understood by all the persons who are saying them.

Now let us proceed to a closer examination of the subject. Here, as an example, is part of a prayer taken from one form of burial service:

Out of the depths I have cried to Thee, O Lord; Lord hear my voice.

Let Thine ears be attentive to the voice of my supplication.

If Thou, O Lord, wilt mark iniquities; Lord who shall stand it?

For with Thee there is merciful forgiveness: and by reason of Thy law I have waited for Thee, O Lord.

From morning watch even until night, let Israel hope in the Lord.

Because with the Lord there is mercy: and with Him

plentiful redemption.

And He shall redeem Israel from all his iniquities.

Eternal rest give unto him, O Lord.

And let perpetual light shine upon him.

Can you, my friend, detect one word which you honestly and truly believe would be of service to a fellow mortal who has recently left the earth-plane for any region whatever of the spirit world? I am sure you cannot.

There is one—just one—sentence which could possibly be of the slightest use—'Let perpetual light shine upon him.' That is the one solitary gleam of sense in this otherwise perfectly inept recitation. Of what earthly use can it be to introduce references to Israel into any prayer for a person in need of spiritual assistance? Most folk will not have the remotest notion what Israel has to do with the dissolution of their friend or relative. The mourners have lost a dear one, and the Church comes forward magnificently and provides them with prayers about Israel. What of the departed one? Is he concerned in any way with Israel?

My friends will understand that I am approaching this psalm-prayer solely from the practical point of view of the matter in hand, namely, to help a soul upon his advent into spirit lands.

Upon the plea for *eternal rest,* I have already made elsewhere a number of remarks. The whole conception which it embodies is another glowing example of the remoteness of the Churches from spiritual realities and truths.

This psalm, which has been treated as a prayer, is frigidly formal throughout. Its language has no application to anyone who is called upon to say it either upon his own behalf or upon that of another. It is sombre and dismal, and guaranteed to deepen the gloom which has already settled upon the mourners.

Death, the Church will aver, is a horrifying and terrible business. The soul has returned to its Maker to be judged, and no man on earth knows what will be the fate of the individual departed person. It is therefore no time for other than the most dreadfully solemn thoughts and expressions. What a world of difference the possession of real spiritual knowledge would make to all these lugubrious recitations!

Another psalm is also introduced which is similarly converted into a prayer, and is known under its familiar name of the *Miserere*.

It commences with these words: *Have mercy upon me, O Lord, according to Thy great mercy. And according to the multitude of Thy tender mercies blot out my iniquity*. It continues throughout in the first person, and the main theme is pursued upon almost the same lines as those indicated in the two verses I have just set down for you. Now this is introduced as a prayer for a departed soul, but the person who recites it is unequivocally pleading for *himself*. Of what use, then, is it to the departed soul, we must ask again? A hopeless plea, in any case, having regard to the falsities with which the prayer is loaded.

Orthodoxy can offer nothing to its members but the mercy of God. To what a sorry state, in good truth, is Orthodoxy reduced.

Then, to pray that God may blot out one's iniquities. If God were to do that, what would become of justice for later in the psalm the individual who uses this prayer promises that his 'tongue shall extol Thy justice'? Wherein lies the justice if an iniquity is blotted out?

But surely the absolute summit of senseless pleading

is reached when, further on, these words occur, *Deal favourably, O Lord, in Thy good will with Sion, that the walls of Jerusalem may be built up.* These are prayers, my dear friend, for a soul who has left the earth-plane at his dissolution for the spirit world, and most probably has been in need of help and guidance of a severely practical nature. The ineffectiveness of such prayers is of a twofold order: by their content they are of no help to the 'dead' person, and they are recited *days after* that person has left the earth world for the spirit world.

Let me tell you of my own experiences in this connection. My passing was in every respect uneventful and perfectly straightforward. During those last moments which I spent upon earth, and when it was obvious that I lay 'a-dying', those who were present began reciting prayers for me. I cannot say that I was conscious of any spiritual reaction consequent upon their endeavours, but that is scarcely surprising for more reasons than one. Their prayers for me were of like nature to those which I have already quoted for you. I can truthfully say that I was not the least bit concerned either with Israel or Sion, in whatever religious or poetical sense those two words were used.

When I had at last left my physical body in 'death' and stood there in the same room wherein my friends had witnessed my transition, what I needed in my ignorance was plain, simple, and unambiguous instruction upon what was to happen next. That help was instantly forthcoming, but it did not come in response to the prayers that were being said. Indeed, by their very nature it could not.

An old friend and colleague, Edwin by name, came to my assistance, and presented himself to me in that room. He assured me that he did not come in answer to any prayers that were being offered up. Indeed, he affirmed that there was nothing in any of them that would bring him, or cause him to be sent, to my aid. He came because he was acquainted of my pending transition through the perfect organisation which exists in the spirit world. He knew, therefore, that my dissolution was imminent some time before those on earth had any hint of it. When the precise moment came, he was there to greet me and help me, when help was so urgently needed.

After a moment or two of conversation, I set off upon my journey to these realms under the able care of my old friend. I have already recounted to you most of what took place upon my arrival here. In fact, my small adventures with Edwin during my voyage of discovery in these realms formed the subject of my first breaking the silence to earth since I left it.

Upon Edwin's advice I took a brief rest before commencing my travels. While I was actually therefore upon those delightful wanderings, the Church on earth was performing a most solemn requiem for the repose of my soul!

Whatever reputation I had gained for myself both as preacher and writer, the ecclesiastical authorities considered it sufficiently prominent that my obsequies should be the best that could be provided.

Is it not strange that the greater one's material—and ecclesiastical—position may be upon earth, the greater will be the requiem or memorial service when the time comes. Equally, the better one is presumed to be on earth. that is, spiritually better, with sufficient material prominence, the more elaborate will be the burial service and rites. Presumably, if it were possible to point to any one individual as a veritable, indisputable saint, most assuredly that person would have such obsequies as the earth has not yet witnessed!

Logically, that individual would be the one person on earth least in need of such powerful 'intercession' as the Church deems itself able to make! The poor soul who needs it most, who is in dire need of spiritual help because his life on earth has not come within a thousand leagues of the 'great' and 'illustrious' personage for whom such solemn and ornate ceremonial is provided, that poor soul is *usually* fobbed off with a few words muttered in a perfunctory fashion as though the person were of no account—which, indeed, he is not in the eyes of authority. He is, in fact, left to shift for himself as far as the Church interests itself.

How do such terms as 'giving a man Christian burial' come into being? There are certain circumstances where this so-called Christian burial will be denied a person. His physical body, in such cases, will be tumbled into the ground unceremoniously, while the Church will keep a stern spiritual silence. The spirit world, however, thinks differently upon such matters, very differently, and in no event will a soul be left to his own devices.

Help is always forthcoming, abundant help. It naturally rests with the person concerned whether that help will be accepted, deliberately rejected, or merely ignored. It rests entirely with him. We do not, we cannot, force our services upon folk who are not willing to receive them.

It is the great ones of the earth who are accorded the most imposing burial rites; the greater the personage, the greater the rites. But for all the religious splendour, the great one can easily find himself in a position in the spirit world sorely out of keeping with the ritualistic ceremonial that accompanied his sepulture. Material greatness is so often thought to connote spiritual greatness as well.

Of course, it may be argued that if the great one is really not so great after all, then the elaborate and impressive obsequies, the solemn requiem, is needed in his case. From which, in turn, it might be further argued that as no person's spiritual status is ascertainable upon the earthly side of life, then *all* people should have equality in the order of their burial service, and that the service in every case should be the most solemn and devout and comprehensive as it is possible for ecclesiastical minds to devise. Just so.

But what is wanted in *all* cases is a complete reconstruction of the whole of the burial service as performed by any denomination. The ritualistic observances that accompany some of them are mere outward display. They are vastly impressive to the beholder of them. If they do nothing else, they would appear to add to the prestige of the Church. The simple-minded folk are duped by such displays; others are harrowed in their grief by the dirgeful solemnity of the black vestments, and the lights, and the lugubrious music. 'Death' and 'Judgement' are brought forcefully to the minds of all those present.

Even while such religious pageantry was being gone through on my behalf, performed, with the full weight of the Church's power, by no less than a prince of the Church himself, and with full choral support, even while this was going on, *I was already in the spirit realms.*

I was experiencing the thrill of my life. With the genial companionship of my old friend, Edwin, I was revelling in the glories of these realms. In simple, plain language, *I was enjoying myself to my heart's content,* as I had never enjoyed myself before! And what was the

Church literally doing for me on earth? The Church, through one of its princes, was praying: *From the gate of hell deliver his soul, O Lord!—A porta inferi, erue Domine animam ejus.*

In view of my reputation as preacher and writer, and the ecclesiastical title to which I had been elevated, to suggest that I should need delivering from the gate of hell was not a very complimentary notion, to say the least.

The answer to such as might feel wickedly emboldened to make any query upon the matter would be that it is impossible for one to know the spiritual position of any individual, and that it is therefore best to be on the safe side by presuming the worst, praying against the worst, and hoping for the best. In any case, the words are part of the order of the service; there can be no deviation from it; there can be no individual discrimination or favouritism.

As to the effect all this had upon me, I can only say that I was not aware of any effect at all! While my physical body was being interred with becoming solemnity—as it is deemed on earth—I was somewhere in these realms, I cannot state precisely where, completely unconscious of what was taking place upon earth on my behalf.

In company with Edwin, who was acting as my cicerone, I may have been gazing spellbound at some magnificent view, admiring the heavenly flowers for the hundredth time, or chatting with some new-found friends, or being shown over some one or other of the wonderful halls of learning. I might have been doing any of these pleasant and most enjoyable things, while a high dignitary of the Church was actually praying that my soul might be delivered from the gate of hell! That same prince of the Church is now with us in these realms. He is my good friend. Many are the occasions when we have discussed this very subject. He asked me, 'What were you doing when I was performing all those rites for you?' I told him, just as I have here set it down for you. He was greatly amused—he could not be otherwise. He thought, he said, he was rendering me such a great service with all the power of the Church's intercession. He honestly felt that, for he was genuinely grieved at my departure from earth. As he can plainly see now, it would have been of great benefit to me had the words of the service possessed some sound practical application to the real purpose in hand, and had those words been said at the actual time of my passing, and not days after.

There is another prayer in particular which was also said for the 'repose of my soul'. It forms part of the usual service, but it is, I am persuaded, the most horrifying of all prayers. Here I give it to you, that you may judge for yourself. You will note that once again the person who says this prayer is pleading for *himself,* while he *should* be praying for the 'departed':

Deliver me, O Lord, from everlasting death on that dreadful day: when the heavens and the earth shall be moved: when Thou shalt come to judge the world by fire.

I quake with fear and I tremble, awaiting the day of account and the wrath to come.

When the heavens and the earth shall be moved. That day, the day of anger, of calamity, of misery, that great day and most bitter.

When Thou shalt come to judge the world by fire.

There is sound reason to believe that anyone *would* quake with fear, and tremble, at such a terrifying prospect.

Here, indeed, is a wordy weapon of fear sharpened

to its keenest to frighten honest folk, and fill them with gloom and despair.

How the churchmen of old delighted in dwelling upon the end of the world! The end of the earth world was the 'last day'. Then would God judge all men; a separation of the sheep from the goats. To heaven, or to hell, for all eternity was to be the lot of all mankind—and still is, of course. The day of anger, of calamity, of misery—and the rest of the dreadful catalogue of horrors.

Here again we have the wrath of God brought into the life of man, the same pagan idea that has been handed down through the ages, transferred from a plurality of gods to the One God. Could there be a more infamous libel upon the Father of the universe, with whom wrath is an utter and complete and fantastic impossibility?

The world was to be judged by fire, according to the enlightened contriver of this choice prayer. Why by fire? Conceivably, those churchmen regarded fire as a mysterious element in which they tried to detect the 'hand of God', a purger and a purifier, and an irresistible annihilator.

Certain it is that fire can inflict the most excruciating pains and tortures. It is consonant with the churchmen's outrageous conceptions of the Father that they should predict that He would, at the 'last day', inflict in judgement upon all men who had 'sinned', the most devastating of all forms of punishment—burning by fire in some form or other, a fire that burns but does not consume its victims.

What a delectable prayer is this to place in the mouths of people who are mourning the passing of a loved one. What comfort it must bring them; of what inestimable service it must be to him or to her who has passed into spirit realms.

When I reflect upon the various details of my own passing, and recall my experiences of witnessing the arrival of so many, many folk into these lands, I feel almost overwhelmed by the enormous divergence between the teachings of a Church that can concoct such prayers as this and the real truth of spirit life. Do you wonder, my friend, that we heartily condemn all such wicked, mischievous effusions as this, the more so as they are employed at a time and upon an occasion, namely, in the burial service, when they can do no good upon the one hand, and a great deal of damage upon the other. For no soul can derive one spark of benefit from such outrageous prayers. They can cause infinite fear and pain to sensitive folk in mourning.

A moment ago I mentioned Christian burial to you. One of the necessary conditions of such burial is that it shall take place in 'consecrated' ground. This means that the ground must be 'blessed', theologically speaking, by a minister of the Church before interment takes place. There is one prayer, used in this connection, which clearly reflects the wild notions which Orthodoxy harbours upon the functions, purposes, and organisations of the spirit world. It even suggests, by the specific request that it makes, that Orthodoxy *knows* how at least some of us spend our lives in these lands. Here is the first part of a prayer used for 'blessing' a grave:

O God, by whose mercy the souls of the faithful find rest, vouchsafe to bless this grave, and depute Thy holy angel to guard it. ..

What a heavenly reward for a 'holy angel' to spend his time in eternity guarding a grave! From what, it might be asked, is the angel to guard the grave?

Again, you will perceive the major importance which is placed upon the physical body after all life has left it, when it is literally *dead*. As such it is of *no consequence or significance whatever*. The real person who once owned it has gone. As it is, it is perfectly useless. Nothing can be done with it, except finally to dispose of it in some way. It is of even less value than a cast-off garment that once covered your physical body. It has no spiritual value; it is neither 'sacred' nor 'holy'. The former owner of it has abandoned it for all time by the operation of a natural law. In due time it will become a mass of corruption, of evil-smelling and evil-looking putrefaction. It is upon this that a 'holy angel', a dweller in these lands, is requested to mount guard!

I would ask your indulgence for bringing this matter forward in such unpleasant terms as these, but I am placing the *truth* before you in the most forthright way possible.

Perhaps someone will ask me: 'Why are you using so many words, as well as so much time and energy, upon what is, after all, a matter of very little account? Burial services have been going on for centuries. In other words, what does it matter? There are far more important things.'

But, my dear friend, it *does* matter, and it matters very much indeed. As to there being more important things, what could be of greater importance than your advent, and the advent of millions of other people, into the spirit world?

I have spoken to you upon this topic before, but you will not object, I am certain, if I recall to your mind the fact that a considerable part of my work in the spirit world consists, with others, in helping people who are newly arrived in these realms. I therefore speak to you from personal experience, experience at first hand, to be even more precise, of witnessing the hopelessly befogged state in which such huge numbers of people arrive here.

They know nothing of what has befallen them, or knowing or guessing what has already taken place, are in a condition of palsied fear as to what is to happen next. They have been taught by their religious preceptors on earth all about the supposed horrors of Judgement or Judgement Day.

At the very least they believe that a frightful ordeal of some nature, unspecified and of unknown outcome, must be undergone sooner or later. It is our work to calm the fears of these unhappy, tormented folk, and try to bring peace and tranquillity to their tortured minds. We have to deny, as the worst of all falsifications, the wicked things that have been attributed to the Father of the universe, among the chief of which we have to deny that any man ever has been, ever is, or ever will be, judged by the Father, and to affirm with all possible emphasis that He has not relegated that power or right to do so to any person or persons whatsoever.

We have to tell such folk that, by their life on earth, so have they earned for themselves whatever region or place of abode in the spirit world in which they will at first find themselves, and that they will find themselves there because that is the region with which they will be in complete attunement.

We have to tell them that no person is *obliged* to remain where he is but that by working he may progress out of his present condition ever onwards and upwards, and that there is *no discoverable limit* to the heights to which he can spiritually rise if he himself chooses and determines to do so. Spiritual advancement is for all, equal and alike; there is no such thing as privilege or favouritism, no catching the eye of authority and so gaining an advantage over one's neighbour. Spiritual progression comes by merit, and by merit alone. There is no privileged short cut.

That, in brief, and many other things, is what we have to tell our friends in distress because they have been so abominably misled by Orthodoxy on earth. We have to expend our energies upon setting right the Church's spurious teachings, if such wild departures from the truth can be dignified by the name of teachings. *We* have to put right the Church's mistakes.

Instead of sending their 'faithful' into the spirit world adequately equipped and fortified with sound knowledge, with facts, with generous information upon conditions of life in these lands, they arrive in a lamentable state of entire ignorance. Do not think that I am exaggerating the mental state of folk as they arrive, for I am not. Whatever brave actions of which a man or woman may be capable upon earth, he or she is faced with a *dreadful* reality (so they both believe) and that is enough to make the stoutest heart quaver a little.

These are, of course, mental fears, and the greatest of all fears—fear of the unknown. Until we can enlighten them, that fear remains. That is why, my dear friends, we take unqualified exception to anything that the Church teaches which is in direct contradiction and opposition to the truth as we know it here. Not the least among these falsities must be included the vicious fabrications which are contained within the burial service such as I have exemplified.

It is in direct opposition to the dispensation of the universe that men's minds should be misguided and misled by such monstrous untruths as those that are contained, by implication, in the prayers that I have quoted to you. The Church fails a man at the last moments of his life on earth, just as it failed him so much and so often before that part of his life ended. It fails him even after he has departed from earth, because it does not know how to pray for him after he has gone.

It is incapable, through its colossal ignorance, of offering one syllable of help either to the supposed dead people, who are in reality in the spirit world very much alive, or to those who are left upon earth in mourning. The Church has such a grand conception of our lives and the conditions of life in these lands that it veritably believes 'holy angels' are appointed by the Father to guard graves wherein are masses of corruption.

The Church concentrates a vast deal of energy upon a useless *corpse*, mounts it upon a catafalque, prays over it, places lighted candles around it, *blesses* it even, while the soul of that departed person might cry out to that Church in vain for the real help he so sorely needs. But the Church is, meanwhile, far too preoccupied with its burial rites and ceremonies, centring all its attention upon a dead body.

Orthodoxy lives a hazy life of speculation upon spiritual possibilities and probabilities—and most of them, in good truth, are wide of the mark. We in the spirit world live a life of absolute reality and truth.

Those, then, are my reasons—in answer to that question of a moment ago—for devoting so many words to this particular subject of the burial service, for the latter is the culminating event in an earthly life; an occasion when the Church, did it possess the truth, could render such sterling aid to humanity.

Very well, I hear it objected; you have made unreserved criticism upon this service of the Church; you have, in fact, demolished it as being worthless. What, pray, would you put in its place? You have been destructive. Now be constructive.

Precisely. Let me be so, by all means. But whatever I do, it is not my intention to set out in detail a new order for the service of burial. What I will venture upon is to present a suggestion or two, for until a great deal more enlightenment comes upon the earth, that is really all one can do.

You will appreciate the fact that for a burial service to be as it ought to be, that is, regarded in the light of spiritual truths, people on earth must themselves have acquaintanceship with those spiritual truths. The truth will thrust out what is false.

No person or organisation with a knowledge of the truths of the spirit world, of the conditions of life here, could ever give full sanction to the form of burial service as it is at present performed upon earth by the various religious denominations. The few suggestions I make to you are from the standpoint that the basis of any reformed service of interment must be that of spiritual truth.

Moreover, I would not offer any formula of prayers, but merely outline a framework upon which to construct. What I have to say may be regarded as of little moment, but I can assure my friends that were some such reformed burial order adopted, as I shall propose to you, it would make a vast difference to the person concerned, and an equivalent difference to us whose lives in the spirit world are closely associated with the distress of so many newly arrived people here.

This is what I would suggest—and I set down this proposition of reform as coming from a great company of folk in the spirit world who have been, or are, actively interested.

In the first place, the most valuable help can be given to a person at the moment of departure from the earth-plane. That is when power from the high realms is most needed. With this great accretion of force coming so opportunely, we can work wonders with the soul who is stepping into another world.

Assuming the normal conditions of transition, where the individual is closely attended by friends or relatives, and where perhaps there may also be present a minister of the Church, then prayers should be said asking for the assistance of those in the spirit world who undertake such work to take the departing one under their care and guidance, and that power be granted to aid their efforts.

Naturally, if the world were so enlightened as I am now supposing, it is reasonable to assume that the departing one would also have some knowledge of the truth. A *brief* prayer earnestly spoken and properly directed, *will positively do all that is asked.* As things are, such a prayer, even though the recital of it occupied but five minutes of earthly time, or even less, would be productive of immediate results, where the elaborate requiem is productive of none.

If my friends would wish to know what would be a counsel of perfection, I should say this: that immediately death of the physical body has taken place, the body should be removed to a proper place set aside for the purpose, away from private dwellings of any sort and where it would be seen no more by any relative or friend whatever. There it should wait for all the necessary formalities to be complied with, after which it should be hygienically disposed of by those who are constituted to do so. Unquestionably, there is only one method of disposal which commends itself to all of us here in the spirit world, and that is, cremation. Let the Churches quench the fires of hell they have so fantastically lighted, and use real flames for an excellent purpose.

Here I might place before you a few observations upon the subject of burial places. The customary interment beneath the ground is a bad practice, for so surely as it takes place, the grave will always be an attraction to enormous numbers of people; it becomes the focus for thoughts and sentiments. People expend time and devotion caring for the small mound of earth, the stone that is erected upon it, and so on. These are wasted energies, for if the thoughts that accompany those attentions should have any effect upon the departed person, that effect will be a bad one, as I have elsewhere shown to be the case.

With complete and absolute elimination of the physical body so that *nothing* of it remains, this melancholy rallying place, the cemetery, could also be eliminated. Ponder upon what could be done with the many acres of ground represented by existing cemeteries today.

If it were felt that some place was desirable as a memorial to those in the district who had 'died', a spot to which folk could retire to seek peace and calm, what better than in pleasant gardens suitably planned and arranged? What better for the purpose than the sites of the existing cemeteries? Were such gardens to be made real havens of rest for the sorrowful, they would do immeasurably more good than the present dolorous burial grounds.

The same thing applies to the graveyards which surround churches. If these, too, were abolished, and the ground laid out tastefully with flowers and other growing things, framing the church, as it were, in colour and verdure, how much would the beauty of the structure itself be enhanced, and what a similarly useful purpose it would serve.

But in both cases, that is, with the cemeteries and

the graveyards adjacent to churches, there must be no hint of tombs or tombstones. My experience of churchyards was that so many of them were a jungle of wild growth; a tangle of weeds; sadly neglected, and an eyesore.

It may be brought forward in opposition that if burial places were abolished, people would still find some focus, so to speak, for their grief; that if they did not cany their grief to the cemetery, and so find an outlet in tending the grave, they would retain their grief within their homes. They would, in fact, have no outlet which the attention given to the care of a grave affords some minds.

There is only one antidote, or better still, cure, for such minds, and that is a knowledge of the truth. When the truth becomes at length diffused among all peoples, then burial places of every kind will automatically disappear. For no one who is in direct communication with us here, and who enjoys the happiness of continued converse with relative or friend, ever bothers to think of such places as cemeteries. To such folk they represent just nothing at all in respect of their departed ones.

But they do know that they are bad places for *anyone* to visit unless one has knowledge of the truth, and so views such spots in their true light. For the mourner they are the worst places imaginable.

Our friends on earth who know us and speak with us do not deal in corpses. To make the matter clearer how could you, my friend, who are reading these words, think of me in terms of a corpse that is lying in the ground, when I am alive and speaking to you through these writings. The bare idea is absurd.

As to any particular form of the burial service itself, strictly speaking, that is, speaking from the point of view of us here in the spirit world, who once lived on earth and who have 'died', there is no need of any kind for prayers to be said over any corpse. They cannot affect it anyway because it is completely lifeless. As well pray for a stone or a brick.

Actual interment could be carried out without any religious formalities at all—and no harm would be done, nor would any good *fail* to be done. The prayers should be concentrated upon the *living* person, and *not* upon his lifeless body. For that reason it were better not to have the 'remains' in the church at any time. Inevitably, minds are led to dwell upon what is beneath the pall or other draperies which serve as a covering.

It aggravates the sorrow. If it be genuine and not spurious, that is, if the sorrow is felt for the departed one and the mourner is not just feeling sorry for himself, then it will reach the person who has gone, and cause him or her distress, thus increasing our difficulties here.

The substance of the prayers should contain nothing that is not based upon spiritual truths. One might enumerate subjects which should be resolutely and studiously avoided as being untrue. For example, any references to being judged or to the Day of Judgement; to the 'last day'; to eternal rest; to the resurrection, to pleading for mercy for the departed, with a few words thrown in on one's own behalf against the day when one's own time comes; any reference to the wrath of God; to the gate of hell... The catalogue could be extended almost without end!

But I have given sufficient, and someone may chide me upon choosing a subject to discuss which is far from cheerful. Of course, it is not cheerful, because the Churches have made such a grim ogre of the whole subject of 'death'. Every man is entitled to feel sorrow at the departure of a friend, but that sorrow is increased a hundredfold by the ignorance of the facts of spirit life. Orthodoxy has harrowed the mourners' anguish by its wicked dealings in hell-fire and Judgement Day and mythical resurrections and vicarious atonement.

It is one of my ambitions to try to banish some of the sorrow and feeling of hopelessness in the presence of bereavement, and in their place to enthrone the truth and good news.

Creeds

There is a passage in the Scriptures which says, *What doth it profit though a man say he hath faith, and have not works? Can faith save him?* Later on is written that *faith without works is dead.*

The question naturally arises: faith in what or whom? Faith in the existence of God, perhaps? Or faith in some particular brand of religion?

Though the Church will emphasise that faith without works is a perilous situation for any man to be in, yet it would unhesitatingly declare that *works without faith* is altogether fatal. That means not only faith in the existence of God, but a belief in all the doctrines as set forth in the various clauses of the creeds.

Earlier in these present writings I spoke to you a little on the subject of faith, but here we have faith of another kind.

The Christian faith consists of a body of beliefs set down in a succession of clauses under the title of a *creed.* A creed would be described as a number of beliefs held by a society to which all must subscribe who wish to become and remain members of that society. In our present case, the society is a religious one, namely, the Church.

The Church's creeds are claimed to be compiled from the Scriptures, with particular reference to some of the sayings or teachings of Jesus.

Some of the creeds are vastly more complex than others, but all of them contain statements which are incapable of explanation. Indeed, when theologians attempt to explain in detail any one of the creeds, their explication is but 'an exchange of ignorance for that which is another kind of ignorance.' The Church has invented bizarre beliefs, supposedly based upon the Scriptures, and precipitated itself into insurmountable difficulties in its attempted enucleation of them.

In most of the Church's official writings the greatest possible stress is ever laid upon faith, with additional emphasis upon *the* faith. Without it man is practically doomed. Orthodoxy deals in faith as in a commodity. Faith is a passport to heaven.

What does each man think himself of the faith as codified in the creeds? What is his attitude towards them? That is for each individual to say for himself. Many will contend that man must have something in which to believe, in which to place his hope and trust. He must have something 'to cling to'. With that we are in full sympathy, but why cannot man put his hope and trust in facts, and cling to the truth? That is far more substantial than the most sublime beliefs.

How many men can understand the various clauses of the creeds? If they are truly honest with themselves, they will admit that they do not really understand one fraction of them, and the official explanations leave them no wiser. Yet they are prepared to believe in something which they cannot comprehend, whose meaning might be anything for all they know.

At least one of the creeds has been incorporated into the general services of the Church, of which it forms an important part. It is recited regularly by great numbers of people all over the earth world. In every sense it is but lip-service. The 'faithful' have got into a state of spiritual somnolence. The prayer-book is merely a means of reminding them of certain words to be said in a certain order. They are usually gabbled or mumbled. As for the creed, it matters not whether it is hurried through or not, for the words mean nothing in the minds of most folk, though they iterate the words 'I believe'.

What of the spiritual significance of the creeds, the evaluation which spiritual truths place upon them? Faith of the kind we are now discussing is wholly ineffectual. All the faith in the earth world, codified into a hundred or more clauses, making whatever claims the compilers of them might see fit to make, and recited by a milliard of earnest, sincere folk, is powerless to effect one scintilla of difference to the eternal truths of the spirit world, and cannot produce one fraction of a degree of spiritual progression or intellectual advancement in any person. There is no law in the spirit world that can be altered, qualified or modified by any faith that is held by any person upon earth—nor in the spirit world itself! Faith cannot alter facts.

People will believe, or so they will claim, that according to the terms of the creed known as the Apostles' creed, Jesus descended into hell and rose again upon the third day. Have those folk ever paused to analyse their belief? Would they believe those two statements in the same way as they believe that the sun will rise upon the morrow? They have no evidence that Jesus descended into hell. But they will say that the probability of the sun's rising tomorrow is so overpowering that it can be considered in all respects as an *absolute* certainty. Could the same conviction be applied to the descent of Jesus into hell?

Theological opinions are divided as to what is the fate of a man who has no faith, using the word in its religious sense. Some say that he will suffer eternal death.

It is difficult to know just exactly what is 'eternal death'. As far as man's life itself is concerned there is no such thing as eternal death. The physical body is the only part of man that can undergo death. In this sense only can the term have any meaning. Once the physical body is dead, it is eternally dead, for no power on earth, or in the spirit realms either, can bring life back to it.

Of course, the Church does not so interpret the words. If it did, it would have the credit for making a profound statement of the truth—a very great rarity! No, it is not to the physical body that theologians are referring, but to the soul of man, the *immortal* soul. Thus, the soul is immortal on the one hand, and can suffer eternal death upon the other!

Theologians declare that man is capable of 'losing his soul', as though it were a possession of which man could be deprived because of misbehaviour, or because he had disobeyed one of the Church's peculiar laws, or because he had proved himself unfit to have one.

The soul of man cannot undergo death, eternal or otherwise, for the soul of man is imperishable.

It may be asked, 'What is a man's soul?' We need not trouble ourselves with theological definitions—speculations would be a better word—but here I will use the word to signify all those qualities or attributes which collectively go to form what one sees manifested in a man's personality. The soul of a man might be described as the sum of his experiences as indelibly recorded upon the tablets of his mind. Your soul, my friend, is just you, *as you know yourself,* with all your particular ways and predilections, all your fancies, your likes and dislikes, with all your inmost thoughts and beliefs, your virtues.

That is the untechnical use which I here make of the word 'soul', and I do so for present purposes only. Difficulties are otherwise bound to arise in trying to explain certain things to you in earthly terms that come within the range of your understanding—and of my own. For if I cannot yet understand certain things myself, how can I explain them to you with any hope of your comprehending them?

The physical body is the *only* part of man that is perishable. All the rest of him is imperishable. However low he may sink spiritually, yet he cannot perish. He may remain in his low estate for aeons of time, yet still he lives. There is no power, ecclesiastical or otherwise, that can remove life from any single person. However, many horrific laws the Church may introduce, the violation of any one of which can, in the minds of the doctors of the Church, bring everlasting death to the soul, those ecclesiastical laws cannot make one particle of difference. It is true some theologians refer to the soul as being immortal, but that merely reveals the confusion that exists upon the part of the theologians because, lacking the truth, they make rash speculations.

The Church has claimed certain rights over the soul. It has framed laws, purely upon its own authority, by which the spiritual state, even the spiritual locality, of a person after death is pre-assigned. 'If you die in a state of mortal sin,' says one Church with an extreme of dogmatism, 'you will perish in hell for all eternity.' The pontifical thunders of the Church—of this one in particular—make no difference whatever to the facts of spirit life. We still pursue our task of helping folk who arrive here in their vast numbers and so many of them in a state of 'mortal sin'.

They seem none the worse for being in that supposed terrible condition! If this particular declaration were other than the trivial rubbish that it is, the lower regions of the spirit world—by which, of course, I mean the dark regions would by now be crammed with good folk whose only 'sin' was disobedience to some petty ecclesiastical law or ruling. It is a pity the Church has made itself appear so foolish in the eyes of us here.

What does a lack of faith involve in the light of spiritual truth? Just this: *nothing*. Faith of the theological brand has no significance at all in any part of these lands, from the very highest and most perfect to the very lowest and most imperfect, from the realms of pure light to the realms of pure darkness.

The writers in the New Testament place an unwarranted and unwarrantable stress upon faith. That, strictly speaking, is not the fault of those writers. It is the work of various people in later times who have introduced so many interpolations into the Scriptures that the original text has become grossly distorted in some passages, wildly untrue in others.

Faith makes no difference to a man's abode in this world of the spirit, nor does the lack of it.

Many centuries past certain of the eastern races upon earth regarded the sun as the visible embodiment of the Father, a representative of Him on earth. The sun beneficently bathed the earth with light and warmth, and enabled them to grow food with which to sustain in part their physical bodies. The sun helped them to keep alive on earth. They did not worship the sun, as so many of them are reputed to have done, but solely regarded the sun as symbolising God. They have been, and are still, called sunworshippers, and are looked upon as pagans and idolaters of the worst kind. They had no faith, as theologians now use the word, yet when they arrived in these lands they were not one whit the worse for it spiritually.

One Church asserts that all that is necessary for 'salvation' is contained within the Scriptures. In fact, according to the same Church's teachings, the whole of man's life in the 'hereafter' is dependent upon 'salvation'.

But those ancient people of the east lived upon earth hundreds of years before either the Scriptures were ever written or salvation ever heard of. Why should salvation become necessary for mankind upon earth only two thousand years ago? Why was it not necessary ages before that time? Later, we will see the Church's ridiculous answer to these questions.

Orthodoxy has made a monstrous and fantastic mystery of the spiritual part of man's life upon earth and, after his dissolution, in the spirit world. It has imposed conditions upon him which it has no right to do. The old cry was heard, and still is heard in some quarters: no salvation outside the Church, but it involved too many difficulties, too many problems to which a solution could not be found. Men used their reasoning powers, and could perceive no logical reason why there should be no salvation outside the Church.

The Christian religion has given itself charge over men's spiritual welfare, laid down a multiplicity of rules, invented innumerable beliefs, as revealed in the creeds, and so circumscribed man's spiritual life on earth that his chances of anything but 'hell' for his post-mortem portion are exceedingly remote.

As with the extracts I gave you from the burial service, so will I treat of the creeds, that is, with extracts taken passim. It makes no difference to which of them one refers—they are all equally ineffectual.

But I would ask you to remember that to be a Christian means, strictly speaking, to subscribe to the terms of the simplest of these creeds and that the

Christian religion regards itself as possessing exclusive rights in the promotion and care of man's spiritual well-being. The Christian religion is looked upon by Christians as the criterion of all religions, and that only through it can salvation be gained.

The first article or clause of the creeds opens with the words, 'I believe in God the Father almighty.'

Here a question at once presents itself, 'What becomes, in the spirit world, of an individual who feels that, for one reason or another, he cannot believe in the existence of God?' There are scores of good folk who, when disaster of some kind has descended upon them, are unable to believe that God would permit such terrible things to happen, because God must be a God of good.

They argue, therefore, that there is no God. No one, they say in effect, could exist 'up there', knowing that there is so much appalling misery 'down here'. One only needs to point to the ghastly travail through which the earth has passed for copious examples of personal tragedies. Whether their disbelief in the Father becomes gradually softened, as it were, and they eventually think differently, it makes no difference to that person individually if, when he arrives here in the spirit world, he still has that disbelief upon him. Who is to condemn him? There is no one. The Father Himself will not do so. *He condemns no one, nor does He allow anyone else to perform that office.* That is a statement that I have made to you before, but it cannot be reiterated too often.

The Church has a fearful fate in store for the atheist—hell for all eternity.

It is not what a man believes during his earthly life that counts: it is his actions and their motives upon which the great assessment takes place. If he does

spiritually well, and yet does not believe in God, it is
his spiritual performance that counts—and always will
count.

Those who find cause to disagree with my writings
will hasten to conclude perhaps that I advocate or
countenance a disbelief in God, or that I attach little
importance to belief in the Father. I hasten to affirm
emphatically that that is not so.

The facts are simply these: Orthodoxy condemns to
perdition the man who professes his disbelief in the
Father. The spirit world, the land of truth, does no such
thing. The Church divides the spirit world into two
regions: heaven, where all is bright and beautiful, and
hell, where all is dark and dreadful. Unless a man is
'saved', he will go to hell. Heaven is reserved for the
Christian, and the Christian, of course, believes in God.
The inference is obvious, theologically speaking.
Spiritually speaking, the inference is all wrong, because
the whole belief is false from start to finish. *Every man
is his own saviour.* Salvation is by personal effort alone.
I am using the word salvation, not in its theological
sense, but in the sense that a person must carve out his
own spiritual destiny, though he will always be under
the care and guidance of wiser spiritual beings.

When the atheist arrives in the spirit world he
receives a shock, but his shock is, in many respects and
upon many occasions, no worse, frequently less, than
that experienced by many a cleric, for, from the
spiritual standpoint, to believe in no God is no worse
than to believe in the strange God of Orthodoxy.

When the atheist finds himself in these lands, he
discovers also that he has made a tremendous and vital
mistake. The existence of the Father needs no proof in
these realms. The fact is evident upon every hand in an
immense variety of ways. The atheist does not require

convincing. No lengthy or profound argument, no deep delving into hermeneutics, are necessary. He convinces himself, and most frequently in the shortest space of time, that there exists not only a God, but that same God is the Father of us all.

The mind of the atheist is not lumbered up with a multitude of complex beliefs. Therefore, he reaches a true estimation of the Father with greater facility. The nonbeliever will say that he does not believe in the existence of God because he has had no proof of His existence. Given the proof, he will say in effect, and he will be convinced. He gets it. Not by our giving it to him, but by the exercise of an intelligence free from an accumulation of false religious conceptions.

There upon he also sees his mistake, and is deeply regretful. He sees something of what he has missed while upon his earthly journey. But nevertheless, great is his happiness, for in finding the Father he has found himself. His enjoyment of his new life is thereby enhanced. It is the beginning of a new life for him in every respect. So much for the non-believer.

What of the cleric, especially one of pronounced narrow views? So strong is his 'belief' in the God of his own fashioning, or that of his particular Church, that oft-times he makes his advent into these lands full of religious confidence. He feels himself secure by virtue not only of his religious calling, but through the protection which he thinks his beliefs will gain for him. The teachings of Orthodoxy are filling his mind. He is prepared for his 'judgement', and prepared, too, if necessary, to seek mercy according to the terms of his religion.

The conception of God that Orthodoxy has manufactured is the only conception he has. His notions of heaven are the usual ones, hazy, vague, and undefined. He is prepared for something; he scarcely knows what. So often have we witnessed spiritual arrogance in such cases. The clergyman on so many occasions has demanded as his right that all that he believed and taught his misguided flock should be fulfilled.

He will boldly assert that he has always done his duty by the Church; that he has worshipped God in the manner laid down in the prayer-book; that he has taught the Scriptures as he was in those very Scriptures told so to do; that always he upheld the rights and dignities of the Church; that he kept the Sabbath holy, and, in every respect where it was humanly possible, did all that could have been reasonably asked of him. But most of all, he trusted in the merciful forgiveness of God, and where all else might be overlooked or cast aside, that at least he could claim as his privilege in being a Christian.

This is not a hypothetical case which I am placing before you, but one which so frequently presents itself during the course of our work here. I have not 'drawn the long bow', to use an old expression.

Now the cleric takes a deal of shaking in his old and peculiar beliefs. Those notions have been with him for perhaps the major part of his earthly life. They are part of him. His shock is all the greater, therefore, when we have to explain to him gently that his views must undergo a thorough reconstruction. His faith is fantastic in the light of spiritual truth; it has no substance.

He sees his cherished beliefs tumbling away one after another as he meets the truth for the first time. The awful God of his Church he finds to be an awful travesty. 'Merciful forgiveness' he discovers to be a pure fiction. The punctiliousness with which he performed the services of his Church he sees has availed him precious little. The only credit that he can perceive in the latter is that he 'did his duty' as an honest man.

Where he was so proud and confident, he begins to feel less proud and less confident. But we strive to give him confidence of another and better kind. We can assure him that all is very far from lost. He inclines to think that it is. But our assiduous efforts will eventually bring peace to his troubled mind, and so, at length, he will be the happiest man one could wish to see.

As a very pleasant reward for our endeavours we have another good friend and colleague to join us in work. He knows just what he went through himself. His own experiences stand him in good stead. He enjoys membership in our great organisation of 'late' clergymen, among whom we number ministers of every former religious denomination under the sun, and of ecclesiastical rank from the highest to the lowest.

Our society achieves something that cannot be done on earth among the ministers of any of the religions— it achieves complete unity.

The second part of the first article of the Apostles' creed is an abstruse one. It affirms belief in God as *the creator of heaven and earth.* That is how the simplest of the creeds states it. Another version is: *maker of all things visible and invisible.*

The whole subject of creation, as that term is used by theologians, is not merely difficult. That is a mild word with which to express it. *It is incomprehensible.*

Let us look at the matter from the point of view of pure inquiry. The creeds state the belief that God created the earth. Science has affirmed that the earth by some means broke away from another and larger body unknown. What of that other body from which the earth world separated? It would seem to the ordinary mind one suggestion leads back to another, so to speak, but never reaches a source.

The Church teaches that the universe was created by the Father by an effort of will. The Church is therefore stating something which it cannot possibly know, because millions of us even in these lands do not know. The answer to many problems of like nature remain undiscovered and undiscoverable on earth. Those answers are to be found in the spirit world.

But it does not follow that they are open and accessible to all who seek. It is conceivable, you might suggest, that I could consult one of the great halls of learning, and there by diligent research find the solution to the problem of the creation of the universe and all that is living therein. In many instances that would be perfectly true, but in so doing I should first have to possess some knowledge of the subject, or else I might be setting down for you matters regarding which I should not have the remotest idea as to whether I was making a correct statement or an incorrect one, a wise one or a foolish one.

I must perforce know what I am talking about before I pass on my information with any hope of your understanding it. I must be able to understand it myself. But not all information is thus thrown open to us in the halls of learning. Volumes upon some subjects are conspicuously missing. Among those must be numbered such as contain secrets which are not for men to know *yet*. The creation of the universe, or how it came into being, is one of them. All life itself is included in that category. The most we can do in the meanwhile is to make our own observations and draw whatever conclusions we deem sound. We are at liberty to think and discuss to our heart's content. Provided our theories do not clash with some natural law, we shall be secure enough.

The second part of the first article of the creed is an easy statement to make, and assuming that the Father created the earth world, he also created 'heaven' or all things invisible. But what real evidence have the Churches that an invisible world exists at all? Literally, *they have none.*

Theologians and churchmen, generally, will refer you to the Scriptures and tell you that *all* information upon spiritual matters, *as revealed by God,* is contained within the covers of that book. Such a statement contains two major errors. The book does not contain all information upon spiritual matters, and what it does contain was not revealed by God. That book is hundreds of years old. Has not the Church something— anything—more up-to-date? It has not. Has it any means by which information could be gathered? It has not.

Although there are means and opportunities of communication between the 'unseen' world and the earth world, has the Church received or accepted any communication from us in these lands *officially*? It has not. One religious denomination at least does not concern itself with whatever its individual members may practice and preach.

To the Church the spirit world might be, to all intents and purposes, a dead world. At least, it is a world of the dead! You will recall the old saying that 'dead men tell no tales.' So-called dead men cannot tell the Church anything because it does not believe that we can speak. It refuses to accept any knowledge upon the subject.

The Churches will complaisantly accept the few, the

extraordinarily few, words that Jesus is reputed to have said upon the 'afterlife', without entertaining the verist suspicion as to why so little was said upon a subject of such vital importance to all men. The truth is not that Jesus said so little, but that so much has been expunged from the Scriptures by deliberate tampering. Not one fraction of what Jesus spoke upon the subject of life in the spirit world has been allowed to stand in the Scriptures. The result is that the Church has been hoisted with its own petard.

The original information contained in the Scriptures having been removed, the Church now possesses none, and has no source whence it could derive any of that lost information. The Church, in short, cannot prove anything, and consequently is thrown back upon guesses—mostly of the wildest nature.

The Church is dolefully and dismally centuries behind the times, to use a familiar phrase. It might be objected that spiritual truths cannot become obsolete. No, of course, they cannot, but spiritual truth is just the one very thing which the Churches do not possess. They have a peculiar substitute for it, but it bears no resemblance to the original either in form or content. The Church is in possession of no facts, but relies upon beliefs such as the creeds set forth.

The belief that the Father created all things visible and invisible is at once open to objection, and very serious objection.

First, of things visible. What of the hideous things and hideous places upon earth? What of those blots upon the face of the earth, for example, the hovels known as slum dwellings? Are *they* made by the Father? Yet the creed says *all* things visible.

The answer is an obvious one, as doubtless many will at once retort. Such disgraces are the work of man, and of man alone. Precisely. That is why the creed says that the Father is maker of *all* things visible. It is, in fact, but another example of the tortuous ways of Orthodoxy, namely, to state one thing, but to mean at the same time diametrically the opposite.

You will perhaps recall the observation which I once made to you upon that particular sentence of the Lord's prayer *Lead us not into temptation.* The Church (I then observed) would remark that no one in his sane senses would ever believe that God could lead any person into temptation. Then why state one thing and mean precisely the opposite? Social and other affairs would end in chaos if such methods were to be adopted in ordinary earthly intercourse.

The handiwork of man is spread throughout the surface of the earth, and is obviously of human design and origin, and equally obviously not of God's making.

What, then, of *all things invisible*? Here, you will say, I am on ground upon which the Church does not tread. What of creation in the spirit world? In this I give you of my experiences, but as they are also the experiences of millions upon millions of other folk here, then you will perceive that I am stating facts.

They *are* facts, and not just beliefs. For you may bethink you that vast numbers of people on earth can believe in some one thing or another, but that it still remains a belief only, because the mere force of numbers supporting a belief does not transmogrify that belief into a fact.

Consider the matter in this way. As I stand, shall we say, looking at the glorious prospect from one of the upper windows of my house, I see around me other houses, and gardens; in the distance there is the city with its superb buildings. Whence have all these come? These are the things invisible of the creed—invisible to you on earth, but not to us here. They are the handiwork of man.

My own house was built by the wholehearted help of a number of friends. It was not created by the Father in 'the twinkling of an eye', by the effort of His will. Why should the Father do what a man, or several men together, can do perfectly well themselves? In doing what they did those good folk earned for themselves a splendid reward for spiritual service, though, of course, that was not their motive. One forgets such things here.

The Father could have created my house—and all the other houses in these realms—of His own will. But we have ample evidence that He does not work in that way. My friends experienced immense joy in the service they rendered me. Would the Father deliberately rob them of that joy just because the Church says He is the maker of all things invisible? Most certainly not.

What applies to my own little house, applies equally to all else here that can be fashioned and fabricated by the skill and labour and devoted care of man. Perhaps it will be said that without God's permission my house could not go up. He did not give His permission. By virtue of a natural law, I became qualified to own a house for my personal use. No one could, or can, deny me that right; even the Father Himself *would not do that*.

I had earned the right to possess it; it was mine, and would remain mine always unless I committed some act that was an infraction of any spiritual law, done deliberately and heedlessly.

Where exactly does God enter in, then, you will ask? Precisely in this manner: it is He who supplies the force, the power, with which to build, no matter what it may be, whether house or mansion, or some trifle measuring but an inch or two. But however skilled one may be, whatever abilities one may exhibit, there is one thing which we cannot do, and that is create life. Whence comes that, it is not for us yet to know. The illustrious beings in the highest realms will have that knowledge.

For all that we know to the contrary, they may themselves, through some co-operative means or another, or some process of co-ordination of vital elements, be able to create life. It really matters nothing to us upon the lower—very much lower—scale of spirit life. We are content to take things as they are, abide by the sum of knowledge which we already possess, refrain from idle and stupid and profitless speculation, and await that day whereon we too shall be admitted into those sedulously guarded secrets. But we can contradict, where we are aware that misstatements exist, since one misstatement may lead to many more blunders, and so help to found what at length grows to be a large deposit of untruth.

In the minds of many people, the unseen world, as they call the spirit world wherein I live, is a shadowy and decidedly unsubstantial region, very religious in general tone, highly spiritualised, and altogether not completely human.

My friends who have followed my writings so far will know something of these realms. They will know that all that we have here is more substantial than anything which can be found upon the earth plane. They will recall, too, my brief narration of watching the erection of an annexe to one of the halls of learning in these realms.

Now that was an act of creation, and in no wise to be compared with the erection of a building upon earth. On earth, men will assemble certain materials, and with them fashion bricks or other components. The process is subject to a formula, but it is without life. But the master-builders and masons here do not first have to collect their manufactured materials before they can commence operations. Indeed, when they assemble for the purpose of erecting a new building, there is no sign, before, after, or during, their work of the evidences which are so familiar a sight upon earth. The substance which our men use for building is *thought*.

The building which they put up is the direct result of concentrated thought. But the thought must have something upon which to function in order to bring permanence, and no man in these lands can do such work without direct help from the high realms. All that we have here is instinct with life, and life can only come from those exalted realms. The power descends and is utilised by those who have requested its descension. In the building operations which I described to you, the power, you may recall, appeared in the form of shafts of light. What would have happened if the builders had merely stood still and done nothing, merely leaving the beams of light to continue pouring down? Would a building have grown before our eyes? Most certainly not; nothing whatever would have happened. But if that force came from the highest realms, or even from the Father Himself, then surely He could have created that building by His own will?

Here we are getting into the realm of speculation. I cannot tell you what might or might not happen; I can only tell you from actual experience what will and will not happen in this case. No building, so I am told, has been erected in these, or other realms contiguous with these realms, of or by itself. I certainly have never seen it happen. Every edifice is the work of some persons whose identity is easily ascertainable. They do not rise up in the 'twinkling of an eye', though doubtless the pious-minded fondly like to imagine they do—if they imagine that we have buildings at all!

Then what of the flowers and all such growing things? Exactly the same applies. The expert horticulturists—and they have to be expert—can form many gorgeous and heavenly specimens of botanical beauty, but they cannot give them form and shape *without* power similar to that given to the builders, nor can they give their creations animation.

That comes from those high realms. In a word, our people can create, but they cannot animate. Creation is left in the hands of the people in these and in all the other realms of light.

You will recollect that I mentioned, a moment ago, of the hideous things upon earth in connection with the article of the creed that affirms that God created all things visible. Now it may be that that statement will be quoted against me, as it were, by reminding me that I have given you some account of, as well as mentioned from time to time, the dreadful dark regions of the spirit world.

What of them, you will say? The same answer precisely can be made. They are the work of man, and of man alone. I could throw back the words to you—in most friendly fashion, of course!—by adding that they are the work of men who have all of them come from the earth.

The obnoxious features of those regions are the result of the obnoxious denizens who dwell in them, just as all the natural beauties of the realms of light reflect the minds and thoughts of those who live in them. In the dark realms there are no trees, no flowers, and as their designation speaks truly, there is no light even.

The pestilent odours which befoul the very air are

but a further indication of the quality of its inhabitants. That is their creation, in so far as they are capable of it. *Creator of all things invisible.* There are theological minds on earth, both past and present, who believed, or yet believe, that the Father would be responsible for the filthy stenching pools that are to be found in the realms of darkness, together with the many more un-namable horrors that abide there.

Why does He not sweep them away, and be done with them for ever? It is not for the Father to undertake this work, but just so soon as the spiritual condition of man upon earth improves and still more improves, just so soon will these regions discontinue to be peopled from the earth.

If from today, for ever onwards no single soul were to enter those spheres to take up his abode, then in time those, whose work it is, would be able gradually to clear them of their inhabitants. With their passage into higher realms, the lower realms of darkness would pass away too. That is but the working of a natural law and such laws will always work thus. The Father does not step in to perform miraculous tricks such as the Church fondly believes He does. If man were to improve his spiritual condition upon earth *before* he came to the spirit world, his own disgusting earthly hovels of dwelling houses would be the first to disappear.

The word *supernatural* is utterly devoid of meaning either in your world or ours. The Father Himself does not act above or beyond what is natural. Natural laws are paramount, and the Father is the great exemplar of them.

Perhaps my friends will wonder why I am using so many words upon this particular aspect of our subject, namely, creation? My reason is a simple one, yet it is extremely important. The opening words of the creeds set, as it were, the key for the whole composition. They purport to set forth the claims which the Church makes upon God's behalf, and from that series of clauses the whole grand misconception of the Father arises.

Lest someone should say 'Surely God does not need *you* to defend Him?' I would reply, 'Of course He does not.' That is not what I should have the presumption to do. One of my great desires is to help to wipe away the misconceptions which abound concerning the Father of us all because once that is done a vast deal else will assume its rightful place and proportions.

When I tell you—as any other person in these realms could and would tell you—that the Father of the universe is a real Father, whose will is that all people shall be happy upon earth and ever afterwards in the spirit world, who is not, who never has been, and who never will be a judge to judge mankind, and who has not relegated, nor ever will relegate that function to any other single person or persons, when I just mention these facts to you from a multitude of others, as *facts* and not beliefs, then you will begin to perceive some of the verbal enormities which Orthodoxy has committed in daring to make such a wicked travesty of the Father as it has done.

The majority of people are *frightened* of God, and that is a most terrible state of affairs. They are frightened of the death of their physical bodies and of the awful Judgement by God which is alleged by the Churches to follow that process. It is fear and fear and fear, with the Father as the greatest inspirer of the greatest fear.

That is why, my friends, I seize upon the verist fragment of untruth concerning the Father which is in any way liable to turn men's minds in the wrong direction in their relationship with Him. I am but the spokesman of a great organisation of friends with the nature of whose work you are already conversant. I speak for them as for myself.

Do you not realise that Orthodoxy is based upon a series of dreadful misconceptions and erroneous deductions? You would if you were to reside here. The day will come when you will shed your physical body, and come to join us here. It would be splendid if you were to do so completely unafraid, with no fear of the present or the future, but with the thrilling prospect at last of viewing and living in the 'unseen' world, as it now is to you, in all its glory, the visible and tangible manifestation of God's supreme will that all men shall be happy.

How far removed from the grisly, dismal prospect which the Churches offer you. After a life of toil on earth you are promised—Judgement. That is one of the most offensive lies of which the Church is capable.

Creeds Continued

After the opening clause of the Apostles' creed which I have given you, the creed then transfers its attention to Jesus. It briefly states the peculiar circumstances of his birth, which are peculiar only according to some Orthodox beliefs, but which in reality were not peculiar at all, being, in all respects, perfectly normal; then the creed goes on to the simple fact of his death and burial.

In this the framers of the creed have followed the Scripture story. But the instant that Jesus has passed from their sight, so to speak, speculation takes place upon typical theological lines.

Jesus, declares the creed, descended into hell; the third day he rose again from the dead. The Church not only affirms that Jesus descended into those regions, but professes to give the specific reason for his doing so. As soon as he was dead, his soul went down into that part of hell called Limbo, says the Church, where the souls of the just who died before Jesus were detained, because they could not go up to the kingdom of heaven till he had opened it for them. Was ever religious fantasy carried to more futile lengths than this!

I freely confess that when I lived upon earth, I, too, believed in this stupid doctrine, but I did not discover the stupidity—or the falsity—of it until I came into these lands to live.

Among the first truths which my friend Edwin revealed to me, in so many words, was the comprehensive verity that the spirit world had been operating and functioning and carrying out its multiplicity of tasks in just the same way as it had done for countless thousands of years *before* the birth of Jesus upon earth.

I say that Edwin told me that in so many words. It was merely a preliminary, for my own peregrinations with him, and the observations which I was able to make during them, demonstrated the absolute veracity of his statement. It was clearly exhibited upon every hand.

That millions of folk should have to wait for thousands of years in conditions and circumstances which, to say the least, could hardly have been in the slightest degree tolerable, since this mythical Limbo is reputed to be a part of hell, that these countless numbers should be compelled to wait for an official 'opening ceremony' into the better regions of heaven, reveals to the sensible mind the really childish conceptions of divine wisdom as entertained by early churchmen and slavishly upheld by their followers through the ages. What useful purpose could be served by such inordinately protracted detention? Literally none.

The economic organisation of the spirit world, for so we might designate this whole vast dispensation, does not comprehend the trivial. It does not deal in purposeless, aimless efforts. Its laws are natural laws, and natural laws do not brook the fantastic. The natural laws of the spirit world are greater than any man-conceived or man-made laws. No purpose whatever, useful or otherwise, would be served by deliberately detaining countless millions of people in regions which on the face of it were anything but pleasant. The laws of the spirit world are not petty laws designed by petty minds.

What precisely is Jesus supposed to have done when he descended into hell, and then 'opened heaven' for all these people? Of what description, or kind, or nature, is heaven that it should require 'opening'? Where does hell end and heaven begin? The Church certainly could not answer that.

The Church would assume that there is a clear line of demarcation between those two places. *From the gate of hell deliver his soul,* prays the Church for its own dead. Merely a poetic notion that, it may be suggested. Perhaps, but reflecting what is in the minds of churchmen, none the less.

What is supposed to have happened after this vast influx of humanity took place? There is theological silence upon the point. The pious would doubtless declare that these millions of living people, who presumably had brains within their heads, now commenced their unending life eternally singing 'psalms, and hymns, and spiritual canticles', and behaving in all ways as the Church fancifully believes that we behave here, or as some of the semi-Orthodox would believe, acting as though every day were a Sunday, and life one continual prayer-meeting!

What a world of difference is there between the nightmarish notions of orthodox religion concerning the 'hereafter', and the truth about this spirit world. They are leagues apart. On the one hand you have all the Church's trivial, petty, freakish ideas about us and our lands, and on the other you have the fact that we are a superlatively organised world, governed by natural laws, and containing *all wisdom.*

There would seem to be some confusion in the minds of churchmen as to the exact signification of hell. One learned scholar says that hell has been defined as a place of 'departed spirits'. That is vague enough to afford great pleasure to the best Orthodox circles. But he takes objection to this definition because hell, when used in reference to the condition of the 'departed', cannot be a place; it can only be a state. The idea of place connotes the idea of matter, and the idea of spirit rules out that of matter. Locality can only apply to bodies. Spirits, as such, can have nothing whatever to do with locality. What applies to hell must also apply to heaven.

The argument is a truly rich one, for it simply means that the spirit world occupies no situation, and we, the 'spirits', are similarly placed. We are nothing and we live nowhere! We have length and breadth and depth, but unfortunately for us we have no magnitude! We might be shadows of some sort but for the fact that shadows do have a little breadth sometimes!

Let us accept for the moment this gentleman's argument. Hell is a *state* only. Very well.

In what follows, my friends will understand that in the minds of most folk on earth the word hell means the lower regions of the spirit world, and the exact antithesis of heaven. Hell is everything that is horrible. In the spirit world we do not specially designate the dark regions under the appellation of hell.

Speaking from experience, my own and that of hosts of others, hell must be a state that is easily recognised from a distance, having a great many distinctive features nowhere else to be found, a state, moreover, which is highly malodorous and can be perceived by way of the nostrils—very readily perceived.

I have clambered over the rocky places in 'hell', seen at first hand the disgusting pools with their reeking stench, examined the filthy, greenish slime upon the surface of the rocks, and observed at close quarters the denizens of those festering regions, many of them habited with but tattered remnants of clothing.

I set out in a deliberate manner, accompanied by friends, to visit these realms of darkness, and I have recounted to you what we saw there. We went from here to there, from one *place* to another, from light to darkness. We went on foot as ordinary pedestrians. We left all our beautiful surroundings behind us, the flowers, the grass, the trees, and the pure crystal water, and many delightful friends.

As we proceeded upon our way the country gradually deteriorated and the light diminished until we were fairly in the midst of darkness and horrors. And that learned churchman would have it that 'hell' is no place—nor heaven either for that matter. His hell is only a *state*. In other words, a *condition* created by the mind, without substance and without locality.

That is precisely what it is not. It is a *place* created by the mind, and that is something very different. For the mind in these lands, whether of darkness or of light, can and does create solidly.

The minds of the unfortunates in the lightless realms have no beauty in them, either spiritual beauty or material beauty. They can think only in terms of brute beastliness, and the result—according to natural law—is grim-faced cruel rocks, surfaced with loathsome slime, rocky hollows containing thick, viscid liquid of reeking offensiveness.

The evil mind through evil deeds will produce the most hideous and abhorrent parodies of the human form and features. I have seen hands upon one of the denizens of these regions which resembled nothing so much as the wicked talons of some carnivorous beast of the earth, and whose teeth were veritable fangs. These were not a 'state'; they were real and actual.

If they were not real, then nothing either on earth or in these realms is real. There can be no reality.

Everything is but a dream; a nightmare, the vaporings of the mind. Let us come back to reality, and demolish that cleric's silly 'state'. Let me give you a simple comparison.

You are reading these words of mine from the printed page, and the words are printed upon paper which, when the book is closed, is quite a solid little affair. You could tap someone on the hand with it, to attract his attention, and that person would undoubtedly feel it.

A number of these books packed together will weigh heavily, because paper always weighs a little on the heavy side. To be brief, this book is solid and occupies space. You would not call it a 'state'. No; I hardly think you would. It occupies space so nicely in fact that you can place it on your book-shelf.

The book is very real, but it *is no more real than any book which we have in these lands*. In good truth, *it is less real*, for it has no life in it, while our books live in their very substance. Now, I have some books on my own shelves—one of them I am not proud of, for I wrote it myself, and I wish I had not. But that is by the way.

Those volumes on my shelf are solid and permanent; they can be handled and moved about, and placed anywhere I wish. Would you call those books and the shelves upon which they reside a 'state'? The question answers itself.

The fact is that churchmen, generally, of whatever denomination, are obsessed by the notion that nothing in the spirit world has any solidity at all. We are 'of the spirit', they echo one another, and that can have no substantiality about it. What they really think and believe in their inmost minds they alone know.

Whatever it may be, outwardly they cannot contemplate either us or the land we inhabit other than in terms of something which is essentially tenuous and vapoury. The reverse is the truth. We are *essentially* solid and substantial. To us our own world and its inhabitants are relatively more material than are your earth world and its inhabitants to you. Among the superabundant advantages which we have over you is the fact that we are imperishable, while you are not.

In contradistinction to the theologians who believe hell to be a state and not a place, we have the opposite school of thought which insists that not only is hell a place, but a fiery place withal. Into these realms are despatched all the folk who have offended God and 'died' in that unhappy condition. The pitfalls are many into which the wicked may tumble. Even the infraction of some one of the Church's 'commandments' may precipitate an unfortunate soul into hell for all eternity, because the breaking of it has offended God!

There is no appeal. Stern justice—of the theological brand. In this hell are *torturing* flames, burning but never consuming. This supreme, exquisite form of torture has been invented by the Father, so it is taught, and fire, as one simple cleric puts it, inflicts the most terrible pains when the same fire is enraged with brimstone! Poor simpleminded fellow, whose imagination is such that he visions a God of love and 'mercy' upon the one hand, and upon the other a God who condemns unoffending human beings to an eternity of burning.

For the descent of Jesus into hell following upon his transition, there is another reason brought forward by other religious bodies. It is that Jesus went to preach 'salvation' to the 'dead in hell'. Some assert that he went there to preach the 'gospel'. The whole conception is a revelation—another among so many—of how far the Church is out of touch with spiritual truths and realities. For if there is one thing which does not take place in these lands it is any thought of 'preaching'. By preaching, of course, is meant preaching the gospel, the Christian gospel.

I have already essayed to show you that the Christian religion is not the spiritual standard of these lands. The spirit world is *not* a Christian world of the spirit. It acknowledges no allegiance to any doctrines, dogmas, or creeds, whether they be Christian or otherwise. It recognises the truth alone, and the truth is the standard.

The Christian religion has a vast deal yet to learn. It is highly problematical that it ever will. Organised Christianity will have its merits, but they are far out-weighed by its demerits. The beliefs of the Christian religions of the earth taken as a whole, and comprising a wide variety of preposterous doctrines, are so far removed from the truth that they have no application to life as it is lived in the spirit world. So that the last thing to be heard in these realms is 'preaching the gospel'.

The inhabitants of the dark regions are not treated in this wholesale manner. Of what use would it be?

The minister who would think upon these lines would, perhaps, bethink himself of some pleasant little Sabbath Day congregation, in some quiet secluded spot where all was peace, and where he mounted his pulpit and drooled along, quoting scripture profusely, and thinking that he was elevating the minds of his flock, whereas, in all probability, their minds, or most of them, were completely blank during the whole procedure. That is 'preaching the gospel', and no one would dispute the fact.

How would that same artless soul preach the gospel to the dwellers of the dark regions here? If by chance he were to penetrate into these quarters by himself, with just his elementary gospel knowledge and an earnest heart, he would undergo such experiences *within the first few minutes* of his incursion as he would never be likely to forget. He would scarcely have time even to draw his initial breath to begin his preaching. In his raw state he would suffer more than he would ever have believed possible.

And what of Jesus? However the poor parson might be situated, it may be alleged that with Jesus it was altogether different. With Jesus it was *not* altogether different. Jesus would not have been permitted to venture into those regions within a few hours, literally, of his passing into these lands. He would have been in no condition to do so had it even been allowed. For no one ventures into the darkness without being properly equipped.

During the course of my peregrinations in company with my friends Edwin and Ruth, in the early days of my residence here, we journeyed to the threshold of the dark realms. We had already penetrated the mist when we were accosted by one whose task it was to keep close watch upon such as Ruth and myself, lest we should wander too far afield and into distress.

This vigilant friend, however, immediately recognised Edwin as an experienced man, and he knew we were in safe hands. Had we been unescorted by Edwin—or by someone equally experienced—we should inevitably have been turned back. But on that occasion we did not proceed any further. It was early days yet. Later, we made a deep penetration right into the lands of pure darkness. Ruth and I were completely ignorant of what we were to find, and of the many dangers. Not so Edwin, who was fully conversant with the regions and their conditions.

The post-mortem movements of Jesus were in no instance dissimilar to those of any other person whose first destination in these lands, after his dissolution, is that of the realms of light. That is to say, immediately after his transition, he was conducted to a place of rest which had already been prepared for his reception, and there he was faithfully and carefully tended. That he needed such care and attention requires no explanation. The very means of his dissolution were enough to warrant that he should have immediate rest and energising.

And it was so. But he required considerably less than many another individual has before and since needed. Many folk undergo long periods of 1llness and protracted suffering before passing here. Besides being in a very debilitated condition physically, their spirit body is reacted upon, and so needs spiritual invigorating.

The whole process in such cases may take a long time as measured in earthly days. But where the physical body is otherwise healthy, although transition has come upon the individual violently, with or without warning of its imminence, the period of rest may be very much curtailed. Jesus left the earth in the prime of his life, albeit his transition was brought about by the most horrible means. It is the latter circumstance which, were other exigencies absent, would cause him to be taken far away from the earth-plane with the utmost despatch.

The very idea that, immediately following upon his departure from earth, Jesus 'descended into hell' is an assumption which is at once refuted by a full knowledge of the facts. It is against all the rules and orders of procedure of the spirit world that any soul, instantly upon his transition, should so deviate from his proper path as to visit the realms of darkness.

A further question arises. What good purpose could Jesus hope to serve had he been permitted to do what the creeds allege that he did? Jesus with all his wide spiritual knowledge would assuredly know better than to suggest embarking upon such an expedition.

That was the first thought. There would be no cessation of individual labour in the dark realms that Jesus should have to sacrifice himself still further. In a word, he was in no condition to do other than he did.

With the best will in the world, he could have achieved nothing for he was in no state to accomplish anything. He could scarcely have been coherent. How, then, could he have 'preached the gospel'—if such an *outré* performance could ever have been contemplated? No; Jesus, upon his passing into the spirit world, was perfectly contented to leave himself in the hands of friends who were there expressly to assist him, and who knew exactly what to do, how to do it, and when to do it.

That he returned to the earth-plane so quickly following his transition, and was able to visit his friends there, speaks eloquently of the efficacy of his rest and treatment. His splendid physical health would be largely contributive towards such speedy return.

After he had made his supposed descent into hell, Jesus, according to the creed, 'rose from the dead.' This, in fact, is the *resurrection*, upon which such immense importance is attached by the whole Church. You are taught upon earth that Jesus was among the 'dead' for part of three days, and on the third day, he 'rose from the dead'.

Here, indeed, is a problem for the theologians to solve, and they have extended themselves nobly with words in doing so. They have 'risen to the occasion'. Knowing nothing whatever about 'after death' conditions, and believing Jesus to be an exception to all rules and subject to no natural laws because they had already deified him, the creed-makers fabricated a preposterous declaration which they could not understand themselves, and then proceeded to explain it.

That explanation, to quote again, is 'but an exchange of ignorance for that which is another kind of ignorance.'

There is another saying which might be appropriately applied here and upon a great many more occasions in connection with this subject, namely, 'What a tangled web we weave, when first we practice to deceive.'

Orthodoxy has been deceiving the earth world for generations. It has been deceiving the millions of earthly dwellers that it possesses spiritual authority that is God-given, that it holds the whole deposit of spiritual truth as it concerns a man on earth and his life in the spirit world. It has deceived the earth world with a brave display of knowledge and learning.

Its chief supporters, the churchmen, exhibit their ignorance under a cloak of erudition. But the knowledge and learning of Orthodoxy, as expressed in its many doctrinal and dogmatic enigmas, and the erudition of its clerics as revealed in the manifold 'interpretations' of those same theological conundrums, are but the sorriest ignorance when viewed in the powerful, penetrating light of spiritual truth. That light reveals Orthodoxy as nothing but the veriest shoddy; the doctrines as nothing but trivialities; the dogmas as the shallow, unimaginative thinking of unimaginative minds.

Upon the resurrection of Jesus a first importance is attached. The Church teaches that after Jesus had undergone dissolution 'he raised his body to life again on the third day'—he raised his body, you will note. Again you have the attribution to Jesus of powers which he did not possess.

If Jesus raised himself from the dead (so-called) by virtue of transcendent powers which, presumably, no other individual possesses, then of what moment is that resurrection? How can it affect in any way the whole wide family of human beings upon earth who are all journeying towards their ultimate transition? Obviously, it can affect them not at all.

The truth is that the death of the physical body of Jesus was in exact accordance with natural law, and in no single solitary detail was it a variant of its operation or in conflict with it, or any modification or qualification of that law. It is these factors which make the subsequent reappearance of Jesus upon earth of such first-rate importance and sterling value to all men.

Jesus demonstrated to his friends that he had survived death of the physical body. He returned to earth to prove the truth of his many words upon the subject, spoken to them before he passed into the spirit world. Of what value could any such demonstration be to the whole earth world if Jesus were himself God? The answer is simply *none*. The Father was not concerned with showing how mighty is His power.

Upon his return to earth, Jesus said in effect: 'I have laboured to tell you that "death" is not the end. In good truth, it is but the beginning of real life. You saw me "die". Here am I, come back from that mysterious place you call "beyond the grave". Here have I come to prove to you in my own person, and by the weight of evidence of my own experience, that I have never been "dead". I am alive; I have always been alive since that moment in Bethlehem.'

That was the true purpose of the return of Jesus to his friends on earth—just as thousands of folk have similarly returned to their friends, and for the same purpose.

The resurrection of Jesus was no 'miracle'. *There was no resurrection.* How could there be? There is no psychic process under which it could be designated. Whence did Jesus rise? And whither? The actual process of transition in the case of Jesus was no different in any detail from that of every other human being. It is precisely the same in every instance, *without exception.*

You will recollect how I have compared your nightly sleeping with death of the physical body, of its being similar in all respects but one. Upon your awaking in your bed in the morning the spirit body has returned to its earthly covering. Upon your dissolution, that same spirit body becomes disunited, never to rejoin the discarded physical vehicle.

Would you describe rising from your bed upon each succeeding morning of your earthly life as your resurrection? Not if you were normally constituted. If you had misguided poetical tendencies you might be tempted to such 'flights of fancy'. And flight of fancy adequately describes the use of the word resurrection in connection with the spirit return of Jesus.

How this simple, easily explained fact of his return to his friends has been misinterpreted, mistaken, misunderstood; how it has been distorted into something it was never intended to be—a great exhibition of Divine Power.

The Church teaches that Jesus *raised himself up.* How could he do that? From 'death' he raised himself to life, presumably in the same way as, when on earth, he is mistakenly supposed to have raised dead people to life. The simple truth is that there is nothing to 'raise up'.

Life is continuous. The death that intervenes is the death of the physical body only. There is no break in life's continuity. One may lapse into a gentle sleep, but the awakening is in all respects similar to your awakening from sleep upon earth. That is such a commonplace *everyday* action that all people undergo that there is no occasion to signalise it by an exclusive name or title, suggestive of what it is not. It is just an awakening from sleep, when sleep has taken place. There is no resurrection about it.

After the so-called resurrection, Jesus then, in the terms of the creed, ascended into Heaven and *sitteth at the right hand of God the Father Almighty.*

The Church explains this article of the creed by saying that Jesus went up, *body and soul*, into heaven. But it is by no means clear which body is meant.

If the spirit body is meant, then why state what is palpably obvious, for the spirit body cannot be separated from the soul? If the physical body is intended, then this article becomes greater nonsense still.

Whatever expressions are used, it is intended to indicate that Jesus went up into heaven.

How does the Church explain that Jesus 'sitteth at the right hand of God'? This way: that Jesus, being also God, went up into the highest place in heaven. Then it hastens to make this truly brilliant and illuminating addition, that the Church in using the words 'at the right hand of God' *does not mean that God has hands, for He is a spirit!*

A spirit does not have hands! Surely Orthodoxy excels itself in this instance of the profundity of its knowledge. God has no hands, for He is a spirit. Therefore, no spirits have hands.

Of what nature does the Church believe us to be? If

we have no hands, can we possibly have feet? Why this selective preference in favour of the rest of the body at the expense of the hands?

The hands are such indispensable limbs. One can do much more, comparatively speaking, under the absence of feet than one could under the absence of hands. If no hands, what of the rest of the body?

There seems to be no rational reason why hands should be thus victimised, if I may so express it. Logically, if no hands, then no other limbs? So what becomes of us?

We are reduced to nothing. A body must have its parts or it is no body; just a mere hulk. Perhaps the Church imagines that we are but trunks with a head superimposed. What monsters we must be. The outward appearance which we present to all people must be rather repulsive.

But I can see no other conclusion to draw but that if we have no hands it speaks pretty poorly for our having any other limbs. For a life of complete and utter idleness, such as is envisaged in the prayer for 'eternal rest', hands would be redundant.

It is difficult to think that those wonderful hands of Jesus, those hands that did so much good to suffering souls upon earth with their healing, should no longer be part of the same great soul.

Of course, my friends, all this is too childish for words. Let us return to sense and sanity.

We are, in every respect, provided with our full complement of limbs. We are not monstrosities here in these realms of the spirit world. We each have our respective work to do; we use our hands and limbs just as you do on earth, and for the same purposes.

Without hands, how could I open a door, for instance,

or move the contents of my home about, or perform the hundreds of kindred actions that all come 'in the day's work'?

Jesus is like the rest of us in this respect. To suggest that he has no hands would be grossly insulting if it were not for the fact that such a belief were mere childishness.

But it does reveal the condition of abysmal ignorance into which the Church is plunged, the Church that claims for itself the office of spiritual guide, claims that it has the whole deposit of spiritual truth.

One denomination, the very same that is responsible for the 'explanation' of the missing hands of Jesus, claims to be infallible. One can readily judge the quality of its infallibility by the sample which I have just give you.

It infallibly teaches that a spirit cannot have hands! Let that Church try to explain such a statement—if it can. Assuredly it cannot—without floundering into a muddle of words which in the end mean nothing and leave the enquirer no wiser.

My friends will not wonder why it is we in the spirit world think so poorly of the Churches and their teachings. If by chance any minister of the Church were to see us in the semblance which the Church fondly teaches to be ours, he would be either frightened out of his wits, or revolted by the spectacle, and thereupon pronounce us as devilish because we were limbless misshapen monsters.

Creeds Concluded

After Jesus had ascended into heaven, the creed declares that 'from thence he shall come to judge the living and the dead.'

My friends will be familiar with what I have already said upon this fallacious doctrine. At the same time I would wish that there should be no mistake about it. I have told you that at no time does the Father judge any man. He has never done so, and He will never do so. What is just as important, He has not relegated, nor will He ever relegate, that office to any person whatsoever. It must not be forgotten that in the eyes of Orthodoxy Jesus is God.

As the claims of the creed stand it is Jesus, as God, who will judge all men.

Let me put the matter to you in this way. If this doctrine be true, then there is nothing more to be said. If it is not true—*and it is not true*—what, to put the question in plain words, what is the opinion of the spirit world upon it, and still more, what is the opinion of Jesus himself? Indeed, many of my friends of earth might be tempted to ask: 'Where is Jesus? Have you and others in your realms seen him? Or does he only remain in those exalted realms wherein one supposes he abides?'

To answer the last questions first: there is no one of us in these realms who has not seen Jesus himself. He is a constant visitor, and it has been my privilege, as well as that of many another, to have spoken with him. And why not, pray? There is no bar or barrier, no hindrance of any kind, to a being of the exalted realms visiting any lower realm he so chooses. Visitants from the high realms are continually to be observed upon their journeyings to and fro between their own spheres and these and other spheres. They have work to do which takes them upon visits in person.

Such beings know the infinite delight they afford us here by their presence, and they do not deny us that pleasure merely because someone—or anyone—does not think they can or should journey from their high estate to a lower realm. We are not subject to earthly opinions in such matters: we acknowledge realities— the realities of the spirit world.

With the universal prominence of the very name of Jesus, it is not remarkable that we should seek the opportunity of seeing him and speaking with him. What do you suppose are the feelings of folk when, meeting Jesus in this natural way, they recall what their Church taught them about him while they were incarnate, namely, that this same illustrious man and gentle soul was to be their judge?

Perhaps some of us will recall that the Church had the audacity to put into the mouth of Jesus the very words with which he would condemn human beings to hell, *'Depart from me, you cursed, into everlasting fire, which was prepared for the devil and his angels.'* Those words are to be found in the Scriptures for all to see and read.

The Church bases its authority for such wicked teachings upon those same Scriptures, verily believing that Jesus, as God, will pronounce that vicious and diabolic malediction upon erring man. To recall those words in the presence of Jesus, who could not find it in his heart to condemn the worst transgressor, is a revelation in itself. One has only to be in his presence but an instant to know that such an imputation is a most shocking and disgraceful misrepresentation, such an appalling untruth, as to make one feel ashamed for ever having countenanced the belief for the fraction of a moment.

Is not Jesus keenly affected by this frightful imposition upon him? Indeed he is. But he is not merely sorrowful personally; he is deeply and justifiably wrathful that after his work upon earth, after his endeavours to reveal the truth about spirit life and how man can gain for himself upon earth the glories of the realms of light, that he should, after his passing from earth, be elevated to the Godhead and proclaimed to be the great dread Judge of all mankind. What a perfect reward from mankind for the immense services he performed when he was on earth. That is one of the greatest crimes of Orthodoxy—and it has many to its discredit.

Jesus taught the truth when he was incarnate. He came as a simple man with superlative qualities; his psychic faculties were trained to the highest degree of perfection, and he used them during his short term of life on earth ever in the service of man.

Never, on any occasion, did he condemn a single living soul for his spiritual transgressions. He did not condemn folk; *he helped them*, always helped them. His whole nature would have recoiled at the very thought of having to pronounce judgement, eternal or otherwise, upon any person. And he *knew*, moreover, that the Father Himself does not judge any man, nor will permit anyone else to do so. That is what Jesus taught when he was on earth.

Any reference, therefore, which you may come across

in the Scriptures that speaks in these terms, namely, of the Father's judgement upon any man, or of his eternal damnation, treat it not merely with suspicion, but cast it aside as being worthless, an untruth, a wicked interpolation by the unscrupulous scribes of the Church.

Such interpolations, if the Scriptures are read carefully, should reveal themselves for what they are. In the spirit world, whenever the occasion has arisen, Jesus has totally dissociated himself from such utterances with the utmost vigour—and doubtless such occasions will continue to arise until the earth becomes more enlightened upon spiritual truths.

It is natural that when we are in conversation with Jesus these questions should present themselves, especially among those of us who were ministers of the various Churches. Jesus has infinite patience, since he must have answered the same questions time out of mind. He forever treats each new interrogator as though he were the first to ask such a question.

When we ponder upon what we said and did upon earth in the name of Jesus, is it any wonder that we shudder? We used his name pretty freely during the course of our ecclesiastical ministrations until it came to have almost talismanic value in our minds. We used it at the end of many of the Church's prayers, incorporating it into sentences which, when critically examined, are found to have no meaning in them. Such terminations are part of the customary ending to most of the Church's official prayers, and have taken upon themselves in the minds of so many folk the fictitious qualities usually associated with most superstitious practices and utterances.

That Jesus should have been elevated to the Godhead is a deep offence to him. The doctrine of his equality with the Father is so universally accepted and maintained that there is scarcely a person who comes to these realms who has not either believed the doctrine or known of it. We all discover our mistake when at last we come here, and our thoughts go to him who has been so misrepresented, who has been so *embarrassed* by the worship, adoration, and the attribution of deity which have been pressed upon him.

The earth world cannot yet understand—at least some sections of it cannot—that the Great Spirit of the whole universe, of every world, seen and unseen, the great giver and upholder of all life, is one and indivisible. He is known to us here as the Father of all. He has no son who is his 'only begotten son', by which appellation the Church's creeds have nominated Jesus. We are all sons and daughters of the Father. Thus the whole Christian religion expects from Jesus vastly more than he is either able, or would ever be willing, to give.

The 'faithful', of whatever denomination, pray to him as to the Father upon the one hand, and expect to receive judgement from him upon the other. To pray to a person as to God is to place that person in an embarrassing position, to express it mildly. To expect judgement from that person is to attribute powers to him which never for a moment could he aspire to, were he even willing, and to suggest the execution of an office which would be in the very highest degree distasteful to him. That is the position which has been thrust upon Jesus by Christian Orthodoxy.

As to the 'saving' power of Jesus, the elementary, crude effusions both of pulpit and prayer-book, as well as of that heterodox individual, the 'revivalist', have taught people to believe that they have only to throw themselves before Jesus to be 'saved' for ever from the torments of hell.

The Church has much to answer for, but never so much as in this spurious doctrine of the deity of Jesus. For in that one doctrine the whole import of the work of Jesus upon earth becomes distorted or obscured. Its true evaluation is so altered as to make it of enormously restricted application, since if Jesus were truly God, then with God all things are possible, so that what he did upon earth must be regarded solely as an exhibition of what the Father can do. Instead of which, Jesus came to demonstrate what *man* can do with divine help.

If the mission of Jesus on earth is rightly understood, it immediately takes upon itself a new valuation, and a very high one. But one of the first things that must be done in coming to that understanding is to eliminate the fallacy that Jesus is the judge of all mankind, as the creeds specifically declare he is. Jesus is the friend of all men, not their judge.

Jesus is not, and never was, the somewhat delicate individual that he is so often delineated both in pictures and prose—and in many of the Church's hymns. His strength of character and his physical attributes were ever of the highest. The story of his psychic abilities and powers, and the exercise of them, is one proof of that. But to be the 'great dread judge' of all mankind—*never!*

The article of the creed which says *I believe in the Communion of Saints*, is one which at first sight would appear to hold out the greatest hopes of possessing some substance. It is suggestive of much, but it is mostly empty words after all, for the 'communion' consists solely in the faithful honouring the saints as 'glorified members of the Church', by offering prayers to them, and by the saints in turn praying for the faithful. It is all extremely negative.

To use a present day idiom, this particular communion is only open to 'one-way traffic'. The faithful are in communication with the saints, but the latter would not appear to be in communion with them. It would be positively dreadful if one of the saints really made his presence felt and known, and thus made the communion reciprocal and concrete.

Who are the saints towards whom the Church shows so much devotion? They are 'glorified members of the Church', according to the official definition. The Church has presumed to know beyond all doubt, since the Church which does the canonising claims infallibility for its establishment and its head upon earth, the spiritual status of the person whom it elevates to sainthood. That is a powerful and—if I may say so—a tall boast.

What is the truth? Simply that there is no individual on earth who can say what is the spiritual status of any person living in the spirit world unless that individual is specifically informed upon the matter direct from these lands. That has never happened in the course of any canonisation proceedings. Nor is it ever likely to happen.

The estimate of the sanctity of the candidate for canonisation is pure guess-work, pure assumption, and pure presumption. After proving to the satisfaction of the ecclesiastical authorities that the candidate led a 'holy' life upon earth, it is then required to prove the occurrence of 'miracles' which can be unquestionably attributed to his absence after his departure from earth.

As there are no such things as miracles on earth— or in heaven—what then becomes of one of the principal qualifications? The performance of miracles has not always been insisted upon. 'Martyrs' for the faith have in their time been spiritually promoted by the Church on earth.

What a blind performance the whole thing is, for the

Church cannot on the very face of it have the least notion in what part of the spirit world their prospective saint is living. The Church would hold that to be in 'heaven' is sufficient. Heaven is all one; though there may be portions of it that are more select and exclusive than others, yet basically it is all one.

Earthly sanctity, as appraised by the Church, is a quality doubtful in the extreme, since so much stress is laid upon being an exemplary member of the Church, whether minister or layman. Obedience to the Church's laws and 'commandments' have no spiritual value when it comes to the great reckoning. While the Church elevates its saint into the highest heaven, he may, in truth, be languishing somewhere far below.

The calendar of the saints, like so much else which goes to makeup the sum total of Orthodoxy, has, as it were, become a habit. The prayers that are addressed to the so-called saints are upon the same level as all other prayers.

How many of the faithful know anything at all about the saint to whom they are offering their prayers? Let them take the ecclesiastical calendar in their hands. Beginning upon the first day of the year, let them proceed through the whole three hundred and sixty-five, noting each day's saint, and let them write down all that they know of each saint.

The result, I am persuaded, would astonish themselves as much as anybody else. For I should be greatly surprised if they knew one single fact concerning any of them. That was my experience as a priest upon earth. The saints are nothing more nor less than a brazen superstition. If the seeker of knowledge were to read about them, particularly about those who were canonised in the very early days, he would be surprised at the amazing credulity displayed upon all sides.

The 'saints in heaven' is a term commonly used among church folk, who feel that those same saints are powerful advocates for them. What is the truth about them? Just this: that the saints, far from being all congregated in 'heaven', are scattered over the length and breadth of the whole spirit world. There is no 'company of saints', for the saints of the Church's manufacture are not all of one spiritual excellence. Indeed, I have been told that on many occasions in early times the 'saint' newly-made was in far greater need of the Church's prayers than ever the Church was of his. He was in deep trouble often, but the Church had infallibly said that he was in heaven!

The faithful, then, may hold communion with the 'saints', but the 'saints' cannot hold communion with the faithful. Perhaps it is as well, for if active and literal communion were to be established with the 'saints' and their supposed Church upon earth, the latter might hear some unpleasant news, some disturbing facts, and receive a well-merited shock to its presumption and spiritual self-satisfaction.

The Church which makes saints has closed the door upon all revelation to itself by the simple means of proclaiming that all revelation ceased in the apostolic age, that, in effect, God has nothing further to add to what He is already supposed to have said in the Scriptures, and that if one should return 'from the grave' to speak to people on earth, then that unwanted visitor is nothing but a devil disguised as an angel of light who is wandering through the world seeking the destruction of souls.

The term communion, as used by the Church, is as vague as it was intended to be. In a poetic sense one may commune with nature by going into the pleasant green fields among the flowers and birds, and there thinking of nothing in particular.

That is communion of a negative kind, but it has as much purpose and effect as the 'communion of the saints'. In fact, one might be far more impressed by the beauties of one's rustle surroundings, by the charm of the flowers and the song of the birds, and so be altogether uplifted, soothed, and inspired, and brought closer to the Father in the garden of nature, than ever one would be in some cold, bleak church praying to a saint of whom one knows nothing but his name.

Such things as the litany of the saints monotonously recited in procession, with its tedious repetitions, are as ineffective as all other such praying-wheel methods of the Church.

The real saints do not appear upon any of the Church's published lists and calendars. There are some notable exceptions, but this can be said of them, that the time of canonisation was not contemporaneous with their reaching a high spiritual status. The latter, in many instances, came long after the canonisation.

The word 'saints' is not one that we use in the spirit world. We are not graded into such categories of spiritual distinction. We each of us live in that realm for which we are fitted, and that is the end of the matter.

Upon some future occasion we shall progress and so advance in our estate; we shall pass into another realm higher, and thus we shall go on. But however high we mount spiritually, we shall never become saints, in that we shall never be marked by name as being of superior spirituality. We shall stand forth for all men to behold us for what we are, whichever realm we inhabit. The only distinguishing sign, if you can so denominate it, is that of the realm in which we live. Personal insignia of spiritual status, such as the simple-minded members of the Church might imagine saints to possess, are not observable as such. Whatever rewards we may gain are personal rewards. They cannot admit us into a non-existent company of saints.

The last of the articles of the Apostles' creed specifies a belief in 'the forgiveness or sins; the resurrection of the body; and life everlasting.'

Upon the forgiveness of sins the Churches are not in agreement, a situation which will not come as a surprise to you, for they do not agree upon so many things.

The Church of which I was a priest at the time of my dissolution teaches that Jesus left the power of forgiving sins to the pastors of his Church, and adduces scripture to prove it. That statement contains two falsities: Jesus did not give any such power to any person. How could he? An utter impossibility. (My friends will recall that I have already spoken at some length upon this subject).

The second untruth is implied in the words *his Church*. Jesus had no Church; he founded no Church, and was not interested in founding any Church. The words which are quoted in this connection were never spoken by Jesus at any time, for Jesus spoke the truth. It is unthinkable that he should ever even harbour the merest thought upon such lines.

Jesus could not forgive the sins of anyone, excepting only that he could and would forgive some personal injury done to him, such as might occur during ordinary earthly intercourse. The ecclesiastical forgiveness of sins is a pure theological fiction. The 'absolutions' which are publicly uttered in the Churches are meaningless and a waste of time which could be more profitably employed in saying real prayers.

I have discussed with you the word resurrection as applied to Jesus, but here in this article of the creed it is applied to you, my friends, even as it once applied to me. Somehow, I do not seem to have had any resurrection, which may seem rather remiss upon the part of someone or other. But I do not complain. I am very happy as I am, a happiness which began when I made my advent into these lands; a happiness which has gone on ever increasing, and will increase still further, for there seems to be no limit to one's felicity.

According to Orthodox teachings, the resurrection of the body means that you will all rise again with the same bodies at the Day of Judgement. The Church which presents this explanation teaches also that all men will be judged twice, namely at death as well as at the last day. You now know exactly what to expect! I have shown you how, in literal fact, a resurrection does not take place, so that the remainder of the sentence is void. It is immaterial whether the same body or another body is used if there be no rising at all.

Once again we have our old friend the Day of Judgement. It seems to be an odd sort of judicature which includes within its provisions that a person shall be judged twice upon the same count, and one is at a loss to know how this is come about. We are none of us perfect; we have all, at some time, slipped back a little upon the path of spiritual rectitude.

Are our peccancies to be 'held against us' twice, then? Shall we be judged twice for the same spiritual indiscretion? That does not suggest a really sound order of things, nor a just one. Or is it that the final judgement upon the last day—whenever that is to be—is for those who have 'sinned' since the judgement was pronounced at their dissolution?

By the simple estimate of the colossal number of people who have lived from the 'dawn of time', the heavenly tribunal will have a gigantic task before it which, presumably, will last for a countless number of years if each and every soul is to have his case comprehensively dealt with and with full justice accorded to him.

Take no heed, my friends, of these woeful forebodings of the Church. You will never be submitted to any fearful judgement *at any time*, either at the day of your passing or at any future date. You will be your own spiritual assessor. The whole matter is left entirely in your own hands.

You will investigate your earthly life's motives, its thoughts and deeds. You will find yourself, after your dissolution, in that place of the spirit world wherein you will be in positive attunement with your surroundings. Worry not upon the Church's thunderings in the name of God. The Church has no mandate, no right, or authority to speak in His name. It is, therefore, in this respect, as in a multitude of others, a rank imposter, a usurper of divine authority and power.

Trouble not your minds with the Church's vain and boastful threats of spiritual disaster because you fail to accept with credulity its foolish claims. Listen not to its shocking distortions of the nature of the Father of us all.

There does not exist such a God as that God whom Orthodoxy has 'revealed' to the whole earth world. There is no resemblance between the God of Orthodoxy and the Father of the universe. They are leagues apart.

The Father is man's greatest and truest friend, *not* his dreadful judge. He is not a merciful God, for he has no mercy to give. Mercy only exists as between men upon earth. He has no justice to give. That is only as between man and man. He has no pardon to give. For that, too, is only as between man and man. He has no great flaming, torturing hell in which to cast poor souls for small sins committed. That is a hideous invention of the Church. He has formulated no petty rules and commandments, the breaking of which will inevitably bring down His wrath upon you. They are the inventions of Orthodoxy and its learned doctors. He has no wrath, *ever*. That is the invention of the same stupid churchmen.

What, then, you will naturally ask, has God to give? This, my friends, has He to give: His eternal affection for you which is expressed in His divine will that you shall attain to the greatest happiness in the whole world. He would wish that you could be filled with that happiness during your earthly journey.

But He knows that that is not always and in every case possible. So there exists a gigantic spirit world which possesses *all* the possibilities and provides *all* the opportunities of gaining supreme and lasting happiness. That superb prospect is open to every single soul, without exception, who has been born upon earth. There is no man on earth who can *alter* that superlative, proud dispensation, either by canon law, by ecclesiastical edict, or by pontifical maledictions: nor by the invocation of a thousand creeds, by the opinions of all the doctors of the Church, past and present, nor by pulpit fulminations of whatever degree of vehemence.

The laws of the spirit world are paramount, standing high above trivial little 'commandments' of any arrogant ecclesiastical establishment. There is no room for the small-minded, irritating regulations which so constantly beset the members of most religious denominations. Cast fear from your minds, my friends.

Always remember—never cease to remember—that entrance to the spirit world is not conditional upon any brand of faith. It is conditional only upon the operation of a natural process. That process is known universally as *death*. But that death is of the physical body only; it does not and cannot effect or influence the gift of life, as it is sometimes called, of the real person, which is you. You, my dear friends, live on and on.

Remember always another sublime and eternal truth: that all the spirit realms are open to the whole race of humanity, and that faith or religious creeds can have no say in the matter. The spirit world is immeasurably greater than all the religions and all the creeds rolled into one.

Keep in mind that the right of entry is yours to any of the spirit realms, even unto the very highest, provided you earn for yourself that right, which none can deny you, by your life upon earth and by your life here in the spirit world after you have left your physical body for ever. There is no religious society or denomination which can guarantee for you, by its ministrations and by obedience to its doctrines and 'commandments', that you will go straight to heaven when you 'die'. What is most important, it cannot guarantee that you will go to hell for all eternity because you have disobeyed the same society's ordinances.

In a word, the Church has no authority from the spirit world for all that it perpetrates in the name of the Father. The Churches through the ages have ever frightened their believers with the savage ogre of hell, and damnation, and Judgement Day.

We, who have come back from these beautiful realms to tell you something of our life and our lands, are oft-times called emissaries of the devil. What the Churches would do without their great *friend,* the devil, it is hard to know. Man does not require any inspiring from the non-existent devil towards evil deeds. He is perfectly able, when occasion arises, to do all he wants unassisted by a 'Prince of evil'.

The evil man has evil friends in the lower regions of

the spirit world who are ever ready to help. It remains with man upon earth as to whose voices he will listen— to those from the realms of darkness, or to those from the realms of light.

When man has purified his thoughts and his deeds on earth, we shall soon observe a great falling off of passengers to those dismal regions—and the whole spirit world will rejoice.

An Average Person

By way of change, I want to speak to you, my friends, in the form of a little allegory, for such I think we might call it. A presentation of facts in another way.

It is not a story of anyone in particular, but of the average person generally. I will name this individual Edward, for that is a sound average name. To begin then.

Edward was a most pleasant, genial, and amiable fellow. He did no harm to anyone. On the contrary, he did a great deal of good in a quiet, unobtrusive way, and promptly forgot all about it thereafter. He enjoyed his life as was right and proper, and used it profitably in all respects.

Through circumstances over which he had no control whatever, he was compelled to take up his permanent residence in a distant land. Moreover, he was obliged to go alone. Knowing nothing at all about this new land, Edward, being a wise man, decided to betake himself to some person, or better still, to some institution which was considered to be a 'properly constituted authority' upon the subject, to learn all that he could so that he might go upon his journey adequately equipped for it, and fully sustained by as complete a knowledge of the conditions of the country and its life as it were possible to obtain.

There were several Ministries to which he could have applied, each claiming that it had received orders for the express purpose of helping all such folk as Edward.

He chose that Ministry, however, which his family had favoured all their lives. You might say he had been brought up in favour of it, since he was born into it, so to speak. Thither, then, Edward went upon his errand of discovery.

He found that although the office of the Ministry was an imposing building, yet there was a musty, stale odour about it, which forcibly reminded Edward of graveyards and family vaults.

The officer-in-charge was a courteous man, affable in a restrained way; a trifle pompous and pontifical. It was as though he felt the importance of his position, and was anxious that other folk should realise it too.

He was dressed in black, and wore glasses with very thick lenses. Edward noticed that most of the staff wore spectacles, and seemed very short-sighted; he concluded that long poring over ancient books and chronicles must have exacted its price. There seemed, too, a general air of past times about the whole office, as though history had stood still, while the world had gone forward.

The staff appeared perfectly satisfied with themselves, and content to continue as they were for all time. In a word, there was a limited animation, but no life. Edward felt a little doubtful of acquiring the information he so urgently needed in this haven of antiquity and repose.

He broached the subject of his call to the officer-in-charge. Could he, Edward inquired, give him any information about the particular land in which he was to take up his permanent abode?

'Information—that is, official information,' said the officer, 'is singularly lacking. May I ask what made you come to this particular Ministry?'

Edward replied that it was because his family had always gone to it in difficulty, and he was not very much acquainted with any other.

'As you will know, then,' said the officer, 'we are in every respect a society, but we have no connection whatever with any other Ministry.'

Indeed, Edward was aware of this. He had long known there was no co-operation between any of the Ministries. They all thought differently; they had no great liking for each other; each considered that the others were fundamentally wrong; many made statements contradictory of some other Ministry. Most of them claimed a certain exclusiveness; and some of them, from time to time, issued pamphlets condemning the practices of a number of the others.

Each Ministry had based its policy and system upon a central scheme, but for a variety of reasons, most of which were obscurities which no one could really understand, least of all themselves, they had each charged the others with error, become disunited, and reconstituted themselves into a number of opposed factions.

Of these, two were of some importance, in their own estimation. It was the lesser of these two that Edward was now consulting. I should add that it was only lesser in the estimation of the other.

'Before we go a step further,' the officer addressed Edward, 'I must tell you that once you have departed for this new land it will be quite impossible for you ever to communicate with your relatives and friends here.

'There is no difficulty in getting *into* this country you are going to, but once you are in it, there you must remain. There will be no coming back to visit your friends and relations in person. In fact, all communication with the outside world is not only impossible on the one hand, but strictly forbidden on the other.'

Naturally, this puzzled Edward greatly, because his logical mind wondered why a thing should be forbidden that was already impossible of achievement. He began to have doubts about the qualifications of this Ministry, and whether the authority he was consulting, albeit it might be 'properly constituted', was any authority at all. However, he persevered, left his doubts unspoken, and listened attentively to what the rather pontifical gentleman had to say further.

'Opinions,' the pontifical gentleman continued, 'differ largely upon matters touching this land in which you are going to live. Some Ministries will tell you that it is easy enough to get into it, but that you need a special, a very special, passport to obtain entry into the better, one might say, the best, parts.

'One can get into the less and least salubrious quarters with the greatest ease. And here's a point I might mention to you. The Ministry across the way from us—'

'You mean the Ministry of—'

'Ssh! We won't mention names. Our friends opposite affirm that if you should choose to reside in the unpleasant parts of the country, and, of course, you would be most unwise in your choice, then you would discover that it is possible, so they say, to return and visit your relatives and friends and even hold communication with them.

'If you should decide upon that course of action, the whole of that Ministry, from the head downwards, will regard you as most objectionable, in fact, as an undesirable and have you cast out—that is, if they can get at you—like the devil they believe you to be. Mind you, our Ministry does not adopt this rather unequivocal position, and, of course, we have no jurisdiction over the opinions of individual members.

'Not like our friends over the way, who do all the thinking for their members, the staff included. Officially, we *allow* our members to think what they like, for the simple and sufficient reason that they would do so in any case. That is why there are so many differing opinions upon the subject.'

'Why could not the matter be properly investigated by your people as to whether it is possible to communicate with this country, and settle the thing finally?' Edward asked. 'It ought to be easy enough.'

'Oh, but it has been. Didn't you know?'

Edward replied that he did not.

'Indeed, yes. A thorough investigation was ordered by none other than the Minister himself. The various chiefs of staff went into the whole question with the object of providing a satisfactory answer, one way or the other.'

Edward felt encouraged somewhat with this news. At least, he thought, that whatever the result of the investigation, the situation would be clarified to some degree.

'What were the findings of the committee?' he asked. 'Did they prove that communication existed between that land and the rest of the world?'

'Oh, yes: as far as we understand, the report established the fact that communication exists without question.'

'Why wasn't it made known, then?'

'Well, it wasn't quite as simple and easy as that. You see, the whole position was a little involved. There would have been something in the nature of a conflict of authorities.'

Edward could scarcely see how that mattered having regard to the conflicts that already existed between the various Ministries. One more would scarcely have made much difference.

'For reasons best known to itself,' continued the pontifical gentleman, 'the State had declared many years ago that communication did not exist. Upon what foundation it based its declaration no one knows, since there are no records of the question having been properly investigated.

'I fancy they took their cue from some extremely ancient documents having some remote bearing upon the case so that if anyone should claim that he had received communications or messages of any sort from this land, he was nothing other than a pretender, he or she, as the case might be, only *pretending* to hold communication. I use the word pretending, of course, in its legal application, not in the childish sense.'

Edward thought the whole thing sounded childish.

'If, then,' the official went on, 'our Ministry had unreservedly proclaimed communication to be un- questionably established, the State could have immediately dubbed all the members of the committee of investigation, including the Minister himself, as wicked palterers with the truth, even rogues and vagabonds, solely in view of its own enactments and pronouncements, and in consequence, incarcerated the whole lot of them in jail.

'Alternatively, the State could have been made to look extremely foolish. In short, the Minister and his committee could not declare as true what the State had already pronounced as untrue. An impossible situation, you will agree, for Authority to be placed in.'

'What happened, then?' Edward inquired.

'Why, the report was quietly placed in a pigeonhole in somebody or other's desk, and, for all I know to the contrary, it remains there still.'

This intelligence—using the word to signify information only—was disappointing to Edward. But there were still other matters about which he wished to know.

'Can you tell me something—anything—about the country itself? he asked the pontifical gentleman.

'What precisely do you want to know about it?'

'Well, for instance, I have family and friends there. Shall I be able to see them again?'

'I really can't say.'

Then what do I do when I get there? I shall have some sort of occupation, I suppose?'

'We have no information on that point.'

'Can you tell me what is the country like?'

'I have no idea.'

'The climate then?'

'I'm afraid I can't enlighten you.'

Edward was by now becoming rather desperate, not with the hopelessness of despair, but with just plain anger. He was about to tell the official in the clearest possible terms exactly what was in his mind, when that gentleman turned half away to reach for a thickish book, which he placed upon the desk before him.

Edward noticed that it was heavily bound in black leather. He thought that the blackness of the binding was in excellent keeping with the sombreness of the whole office, the pontifical gentleman himself, and all his staff. Why there should be such a preponderance of *black* was more than he could fathom.

This book,' said the officer-in-charge, 'contains all the official information there is upon the land to which you are going. Whatever other literature you may see or read upon the subject is either pure surmise, misrepresentation, or deliberate untruth.'

At last, Edward thought, he was going to get some information. He inquired if it was the latest book on the subject.

'Latest,' said the officer, 'is hardly the word to apply to this volume. *Earliest*, perhaps, would be better. Still, I know what you mean. Oh, yes, it is the latest. I can't give you the exact date; opinions vary. Let me see, now, it can't be far short of seventeen hundred years or so since it was first written.'

'And nothing has been officially written since then?'

'No, no, of course not. Everything that you *ought* to know is in here. If there is anything you particularly wish to know and the answer is not to be found in this book, then you have no business to want to know it.

'I'm not at all sure but that you should not even *ask*. In the Ministry over the way, they will not permit questions of any sort for which there are not already answers clearly set down in the manuals and text-books, and bearing the imprimatur of Authority and Tradition. We in this Ministry are not so dogmatic upon such matters; we prefer to allow a little latitude, which would be taken in any case.

'It is the general rule of the Ministry that if any specific subject is not dealt with in this book, it is because the public are not *meant* to know about it. Doubtless, the public will find out in due course by going to the country in question and experiencing things at first hand.

'In the meantime it is not for our Ministry to speculate upon things which are not touched upon in the official book. There is this, however, I can tell you. When you eventually arrive in this land you will undergo a rigorous examination as to your residential qualifications. Precisely when that examination will take place, that is, whether it will be immediately upon your arrival or at some later date, I cannot inform you.

'Upon the results of that inquisition will rest the geographical situation of your permanent residence. You must understand that once your examination has been concluded and the results promulgated, your abode will be settled for all time to come. You will be directed either to the better localities or to the worse, or even the worst regions.

'Although we make no pronouncement upon any case, at least one other Ministry professes to pre-assign the locality to which every person is bound to go. This same Ministry declares that there is a middle locality or region to which most people go upon their arrival.

'Here, according to their theories, people undergo a process of decontamination by some peculiar incendiary means, which makes them eligible for the more select quarters. That is their claim. Our Ministry does not subscribe to those purgatorial claims. But it will do all that it can for you as an accepted member.

'All that we can offer you here and now is hope, sir; hope for the best. And we will see that your departure is suitably looked after.'

Edward then left the officer-in-charge and went upon his way no wiser than when he came, and certainly without any equipment for his journey beyond a choice collection of contradictory opinions. His voyage and destination, then, would be a complete and absolute step in the dark.

At length the day came, and Edward departed for this seemingly unknown and far-off land.

The Ministry gave him a splendid send-off—after he had gone. A miscellaneous collection of messages was sent after him, but failed to reach their destination. Even if they had, it is problematical if they would have been understood.

Edward's journey was wholly uneventful. What we

are chiefly concerned with is that he arrived safely and without mishap. He would tell you that of the journey itself he has little recollection, but what he does remember, indeed, what he can never forget, is the glorious spectacle of the new land as it first presented itself to his astonished gaze. He found himself, according to his first clear recollection, standing in a beautiful garden from which he could see a magnificent prospect of country spreading out before him. He could see many delightful houses and picturesque homesteads as well as noble buildings of every description.

Trees and flowers abounded everywhere in a riot of colour. He could glimpse the scintillations of colour from a large tract of water, whether of sea or lake, at the moment he did not know. The sun was shining superbly, the air was warm and fragrant and refreshing. Everywhere there seemed to be the very heart and soul of peace. He could see people walking hither and thither, who seemed to radiate the height of joy and gladness and pleasant activity. He felt that happiness 'reigned supreme'.

Edward stood transfixed for a moment until a man, who was standing beside him, broke the silence.

'Well, my friend. You have come home.'

'Home?'

'Yes, indeed. The house standing in this garden is your new home, and this country is your home, too. You are free to come and go as you wish, wherever and whenever you wish. You are free to speak to whomsoever you wish.

'You will find everyone will be most happy to speak with you. Are you not feeling well in body and mind, such as you have never felt before?'

Edward certainly felt extraordinarily well, though he

142

was very puzzled in mind. His new friend hastened to enlighten him.

'You are more fortunate than a great many,' said he. 'So many folk arrive here in a state of terror; frightened to *death*, as you would say, of the awful examination which you were told was to take place at some time upon your arrival here.

'I must tell you, at once, that no examination by a dreadful judge—or by any other kind of judge—has ever taken place, nor will it ever take place upon any person here or elsewhere in these lands.'

'Then—'

'Just so. What the gentleman at the Ministry, and what all the other gentlemen at all the other Ministries, tell people is a wicked fiction. There is not a spark of truth in it.

'That is not the only fiction of which the Ministries are guilty of disseminating,' Edward's companion went on. 'One might ask, what have they of the truth? The answer: next to nothing. What do they know about this very land in which you have now come to live? The answer again is *nothing*.'

Edward was in full agreement. He recounted his experiences at the Ministry concerning the subject of communication.

'The relative importance of the *truth* of communication cannot be exaggerated,' said his friend, 'since so much depends upon it. Without the means of communication this land is shut off and cut off from every other land.'

'Then it does exist?'

'Of course, my dear friend, it exists. It always has existed, and it always will exist. Where you have just come from the Ministries are mostly in agreement that it is not possible for us to communicate. Consequently the whole service is carried on by earnest folk who are not, in the eyes of the various Ministries, "properly constituted authorities," but they are very much *authorities*, none the less, and their constitution has the whole weight of the support of this land.

'There are difficulties, naturally, but the greatest of them is not so much in the process of transmission of messages as in the ultimate reception of them by the person or persons chiefly concerned.

'For instance, I know that, now you have learned that communication exists, you feel the urge to rush back and tell someone all about this country even on so short acquaintance with it, some friend, or your family, perhaps. Isn't that so?' Edward admitted it at once.

'We could get the message through for you. There would not be any great difficulty about that. We have many good agents who would willingly help us on your behalf. But whom have you among those you have left behind who would accept the message as being from you?

'There are learned ministerial gentlemen in the land you have just vacated who have many distorted views upon this land. They really think that as soon as an individual reaches us here, he becomes changed almost in the "twinkling of an eye"; that he ceases to be himself, natural and normal, and becomes frightfully serious, both in mind and speech. That is what they believe ought to happen. Do you, my friend, feel in any way changed intellectually, if I may so express it?'

'Not in the least.'

'No, of course not—nor is it observable outwardly. Your speech is such as any ordinary person would employ, without silly affectations. As you travel about here you will find we are all like that. We do not speak to one another as though we were addressing an ecumenical council, or a board-meeting, or a gathering of scientists.

'Those who *were* affected soon abandon their affectations when they come here, and so become *normal* like the rest of us. You may have observed on your visits to any of the Ministries before you came here to live, that those in authority were, so to speak, perceptibly tinctured by their position and authority.

'Without wishing to be unkind, I should say that their official status has so worked upon their personalities that they have become formal and strained and unnatural even in their very mode of speech. They have grown too weighty, not all of them, of course, but the vast majority of them.

'These Ministers believe that a certain stiffness—pompousness, even—and formality is in strict consonance with their high office. They live, in fact, altogether in a world of their own creation, an unnatural world. They forget or overlook the rest of the folk who are also living their lives, but living them in a natural manner.

'These official gentlemen are unaware of their eccentricities in this respect. So they think that we in this land should be in most respects similar to themselves. We are not. Why should we be? Here we are truly ourselves without any silly affectations or shams.

'It just happens that from time to time messages and communications from our lands have come to their notice. And what is their verdict upon them in most cases? That they are in their content and their very language "petty" and "trivial".

'They positively believe—or they profess to believe—that *all* messages from these lands should be of the highest literary quality, comparable only with the best writers in their own land; they believe that the senders of these messages—assuming, in rare cases, their veridical nature—should only speak upon the weightiest matters, and presumably in the involved terms of their own Ministries' chronicles, documents, and decrees.

'It is because the "alleged" messages do not come up to the standards set up by themselves that they refuse to believe that they are authentic messages, and therefore they say that there is no evidence that communication exists at all.

'They simply cannot grasp that the people in this land talk in a straight forward unassuming manner, using words and phrases that anyone can understand, and dealing with matters well within the comprehension of all. It is a great pity they can't grasp that, but we in this land cannot alter ourselves, our personalities, just to humour a few pompous and mistaken gentlemen in the Ministries.

'There is, too, the wider issue which these same gentry either ignore, overlook, or refuse to accept, regarding this personal change.

'Suppose, my friend, you decide to send a message to your family, presupposing, at the same time, that they would be willing to accept a message as coming from you. You would naturally frame your message, things being as they are, in such a manner that it would contain some personal reference which would serve to establish your identity to the complete satisfaction of your family.

'But were you to employ words and phraseology such as our friends of the Ministries deem alone fitting as emanating from this land, what would your relatives think? They would be urged to remark that while the content of the message was itself sound, yet it couldn't be you who sent it or gave it, because *you* never spoke in that strange manner.

'In plain language they would say: "That's not Edward. He never talked like that." They would be undeniably right, for who could be better judges than your own kindred?

'The gentlemen at the Ministries regard this as a small and insignificant point upon which to fasten, but it's neither the one nor the other. It's a vastly important and highly significant *fact*, because it demonstrates the continuance in this land of personality. It shows that no instantaneous transformation takes place upon a person's entry into these lands.

'People do not become skilled and gifted rhetoricians, eloquent speakers, and literary geniuses immediately upon entry here. What is most important, folk do not become transformed out of all resemblance to their former selves simply by virtue of their arrival in this country.

'Changes do ultimately take place, but not such as our ministerial friends visualise.

'No, friend Edward, you haven't in any degree changed, and your family wouldn't expect you to have done so, were they to give the matter a little thought. But the Ministry you consulted would have expected you to have altered very much indeed.'

Edward turned to his companion. 'There's one thing I should like,' he said.

'What is that?'

'I should like to have that fellow at the Ministry with me now—for just five minutes.'

Edward's friend smiled. 'Yes,' he observed, 'a lot can be done in five minutes. But don't concern yourself about him and his colleagues, or the Ministers and their *colleagues.* There are plenty of them here if you would like to have a chat with some of them.

'You'll find they are much more human and understanding since they came to take up their residence here. You see, they *have* changed. They are themselves, which they never were before. An alteration for the better. The Ministries want to have people changed here, but they never dreamed that the biggest change would come in their own folk! Possibly, if some of them returned to speak, they wouldn't be recognised by their former colleagues!'

Edward was wrathful that so much knowledge and information had been withheld from him, and he expressed his feelings very openly and freely to his companion.

The latter observed that the Ministry had not withheld anything from him; it was simply that they did not know. But that did not absolve them, since the knowledge is available for all who seek it. It was nothing less than fantastic, in a world that claims to have progressed, Edward's friend continued, that 'authorities' should establish themselves for the sole purpose of guiding others when those same alleged authorities were entirely devoid of any qualifications for the task.

'Look about you,' he said, 'and what do you see? A perfect country whose verdure, as with all else, is incomparable with anything you have left behind you. Trees, flowers, grass, of every description flourishing in a perfection of both place and climate.

'Look at the buildings. Have you ever seen anything to match them? Look, too, at the folk here. Do they not appear splendid in health and temper? Don't their very faces reveal the happiness which is ours here—and which is yours also, my friend, for the having?

'Yet the Ministries decree that no knowledge of all these beauties and splendours must be allowed to leak out and penetrate into the land you have just vacated, because it would not be right and proper for it to do so. Did you ever hear such arrant nonsense!

'They allege that the people there are not meant to know anything about us here. Why not, pray? They allege, in effect, that the Ruler of this land is a tyrant. He is not. Does not the very land here, with all the outward and compelling signs of happiness and prosperity and well-being, reveal directly the opposite?

'What lamentable blindness assails the Ministries and all their officials and representatives! Instead of working hand in hand with us here, helping us with their vast organisations, they represent one of the biggest obstacles it is possible to throw in the path of *our* organisations and functions.

'They could do so much good; they could be of such tremendous benefit to the whole of humankind were they to possess themselves of the truth about us and our lands here. They could, if they would, assist all folk upon their departure for these realms with sure and certain knowledge of the conditions of life here.

'All they can do is offer people a "sure and certain *hope*" of something which they really can't explain—a worthless article, for how can hope be either certain or sure?

'The Ministries are specialists in the art of dealing in—and with—phrases that mean nothing. They cover their ignorance with a peculiar jargon, and their ignorance seems invincible. Self-designated authorities who have no knowledge.

'Would ever such a situation be tolerated in any branch of human activity other than this ? Of course not, because those responsible for it would be found out before they had proceeded very far, and branded for the imposters which they were.

'They work in the dark because they are totally blind. They cannot see the results of all their false claims; they cannot see the state of woeful ignorance in which their people, the people they have professed to guide, arrive in this country.

'All that, my friend, has to be set right here, just as I am doing now for you. Here is this beautiful land awaiting to be explored and enjoyed by you, but before you can do that I must explain to you its simple existence. I must calm any fears you might have that a frightful examination is going to take place to determine your "residential qualifications".

'So many people are terror-stricken, poor souls, by the dreadful unknown prospect which they have been led to believe awaited them here. Do you not now feel with all the certitude in the world that *nothing* that was not designed to make you personally happy, could ever happen here? I know that you do. And you are right. So whatever doubts or small fears you may have, my dear friend, cast them aside, and enjoy your new life and its attendant happiness to the full.

'And here, if I mistake not, are some few friends come to bid you welcome. They have not intruded so far because it was best that I should speak with you first, to explain these things to you, for I have been given the pleasant task of being your guardian, and extending every assistance to make you feel fully at home here.'

Edward was overjoyed to meet once again many friends who, having departed for this land, had never been heard of again.

There, I think, we will leave Edward in the enjoyment of his new life. And here I, too, must leave you for a time. There is much that still remains to tell you, and I am very conscious of your thoughts upon many and divers themes which you desire that we should discuss together. Opportunities for doing so will present themselves in due season. and we shall take full advantage of them.

In the meantime, as to our present writing there is one last consideration which I should like to place before you. That is, to remember that when I was upon earth I was a priest of the Church, who taught and disseminated many false doctrines.

If I were the only person to have done that, little harm might have been done, but there are thousands upon thousands of us here in the spirit world similarly placed. It was our life's work to support what is not true. We support now only what is true.

The cleavage between the truth and untruth is so great, and it affects so many people still upon earth, that we who have caught the eye of you who are yet incarnate, are deeply anxious to use what opportunities and powers we may possess to pass on to you the truth about life, for of life there is no death.

Life is continuous, without pause, without the fraction of a moment's break.

We who are living in these realms are *without fear* of any kind. Just think what that means, my friends. You, too, need have no fear. If by speaking plainly and speaking only that which is true, I can help to cast out that fear from you, then I shall not have written altogether in vain.

Why should you have fear? There is no reason whatever. But there is cause for it, and that cause is rooted in generations of false teachings. Accept the truth, for it is altogether far better, far more splendid than anything which Orthodoxy has to offer.

Be not misled by any 'holy mysteries'—the Churches have mysteries in abundance, but they are not holy ones.

The truth of life in the spirit world is as simple as ABC, as one day it will be your happy fortune to discover for yourself.

And now, once more do I say to you with all my heart,

Benedicat te omnipotens Deus.

www.ingramcontent.com/pod-product-compliance
Lightning Source LLC
LaVergne TN
LVHW051126080426
835510LV00018B/2256